LIFE
DISARRANGED

A Poetic Journey through Heartbreak & Anguish

SABITA MISHRA

Publish@nowscpress.com
www.PublishWithNOW.com
@nowscpress

Ordering Information:

    Quantity sales. Special discounts are available on quantity purchases by corporations, associations, and others. For details, contact the publisher at the address above.

    Orders by U.S. trade bookstores and wholesalers. Please contact: NOW SC Press: Tel: (813) 970-8470 or visit www.PublishWithNOW.com

Printed in the United States of America
First Printing 2021
ISBN: 978-1-7369388-0-5

This book is part memoir. It reflects the author's present recollections of experiences over time. Some names and characteristics have been changed or omitted and some events have been compressed.

I would like to dedicate this book to my father Chaturanan Mishra and to my dear friend John Shettle, both of whom passed away after their long battle with cancer. I would also like to thank Father Kevin Downey, Harriet Learson, and my publishing team at NOW Publishing who helped me tremendously to make my dream come true.

Contents

Foreword

JOHN MET SABITA in 2019 at the homeless shelter in St. Petersburg. He was immediately affected by both her poetry and her life story. I imagine it's hard not to be affected when someone has overcome as much as Sabita has and still lives life with such joy and hope. John knew how passionate Sabita was about the possibility of publishing her poems, so in May of 2020 he contacted NOW Publishing to talk about how he might help in that endeavor. The initial meeting in June went well, and John became increasingly enthusiastic about taking up Sabita's mantle to get her poems published.

John was a quiet supporter of many charities and homeless centers. He spent many Saturday's driving to Williams Park in St. Petersburg to hand out sundries to the homeless people there. He'd engage them in conversation and would come home with the stories of the people he'd met. Sabita, though, was one of his favorite people.

1

He knew that she had become homeless through a series of tragedies and felt that being able to publish her poems would bring her an enormous sense of pride and accomplishment after the heartbreak she had endured for so long. Unfortunately, John wasn't able to see Sabita's dream come true as he passed away in September of 2020. I know that he is looking down on us, pleased that he was able to have even a small role in the creation of this book.

I am positive that you will be moved by Sabita's journey, and also influenced by her perpetual hope and enduring faith. Sabita rightly points out in this book that our friends can become our family and that life might be a little easier if we were all to act with kindness toward each other. It was a gift to be a part of John's life and his goals of paying it forward, and it has also been a gift to watch Sabita reach her goal of becoming a published poet. We hope you enjoy.

– Abbey Smith, widow of John Shettle, Jr.

I Believe

I believe in love
I believe in miracles
I believe in God
And everything beautiful
I believe in heaven
I believe in heaven on earth
I believe in random acts of kindness
And strangers who are meant for each other
I believe in white Christmas
I believe that God listens to our prayers
I believe that when we choose to believe
Good things will happen and we will persevere
I believe every new day is about new beginnings
I believe happiness comes when we have faith and it's healing
I believe life is about hope and new reasons
I believe life is about new promises it brings with it every new season
I believe every cloud has a silver lining
I believe in raindrops from the skies are falling
I believe in sun rising every morning
I believe in a beautiful smile making this world so so amazing
Share

Part One

Chapter One

Courage, Strength, and the Unknown

IF I HAD known as a naïve twenty-one-year-old newlywed that the path of my life would bring me to where I am today, I don't think I would have believed it. Unfortunately, I've learned over the last few decades how unkind the world can be. Sitting in the computer room at the homeless shelter, where I currently find myself, I try to block out the noise in the hallway. The drug addicts and alcoholics that yell and scream, distracting me from remembering everything fully. Reliving is its own painful and exhausting experience. I realize how much heartbreak and pain there has been; the different facets of human faces and inhuman behavior are beyond anything most of us can imagine. The opposite of that pain, of course, is love. That was a feeling I knew growing up in India and even the first few years of my marriage. In this moment, it's hard not to let my thoughts go back to the beginning of this journey, to the day when I first met my husband.

A little background on the marriage culture I was born into would be helpful first. I was raised in a strict Brahmin family, and I was well aware of the marriage system. In India, we don't call it "arranged marriage." We have marriage and "love marriages." Practically everyone around me was married by the Western version of an "arranged marriage," including my own parents. As a girl, I knew that one day I would have to get married and I never questioned this philosophy.

My parents were a very strong influence on me as to what a strong and happy marriage looks like and what marriage is supposed to mean. They married young and loved and cared about each other very much; they were happy with each other—despite life's usual ups and downs—and were married for a total of forty-eight years before my father passed away. With their strong model of marriage, the ingrained message that was part of my psyche—as well as my conscious—I was not opposed to the idea. I knew they were still a success as far as world divorce rates statistics go, despite being a Hindu custom since practically the beginning of time.

However, in 1988 when I was becoming of marriageable age, India was already very strongly influenced by Western thoughts and culture, both because of the media and private schools in India. These schools were often referred to as "Convent schools," because they belonged to one of the Christian denominations. Most upper middle-class family's children attended a school like this in in India. I had attended one, too, considered one of the best Catholic schools not only in my hometown but also one of the highest ranked in the entire state of Bihar. There I had been introduced to many Western ideals and was taught to be an independent thinker—to think out of the box. The hope was that we would go out in the world to become leaders of tomorrow.

Being teenagers, though, these new ideas also made us question and challenge some of the traditional concepts and ideas that we grew up within Hindu culture. These concepts are typically firmly rooted in strong Hindu traditions as opposed to math and science, logic, and reason. Arranged marriages were one of our favorite rebellious causes. We had seen too many movies, read too many books, seen too many images of people falling in love on their own to want to have a partner chosen for us.

It was with these conflicting ideas in my head that I met my husband. He and his niece lived in America, but her family wanted a very traditional Brahmin wedding in India. Including all of the Brahmin customs and traditions of our community would have been too difficult a task in America, so the decision was made to have the wedding ceremony at her uncle's home in Bihar. My family was very good friends of his family, so we were invited to attend the three-day grand ceremony and festivities. I met my husband there, for the first time, and his entire family, and they got a chance to meet my family.

In India, arranged marriage systems are the standard in Brahmin communities like ours. It's typical of families to meet like this at weddings, looking for suitable matches. It's also an opportunity for families to get to know each other, especially when they are distant relatives of friends living in very far away cities, or as it was in my case, in America. Brahmin communities are community-based and are always trying to make strong alliances and networks, not only as a way to build personal friendship within the community, but also in a way that emphasizes "good families" and continuing the ever-controversial caste systems and hierarchy. This is especially true within well-to-do and powerful families.

After this initial meeting between my husband and me, both our family members also took an interest in each other and gave marriage between the two of us serious consideration. A favorite saying in India is that "marriages are made in heaven." That being the ancient wisdom, many elders and family members had to consult to determine if we would be a suitable match. My husband's family mulled over the prospect of he and I getting married for a few days, then a couple of days later, the senior members of his family—namely his older sister and his brother-in-law—came to my parents' house in India with a marriage proposal. My parents were very flattered that the proposal was from a very respectable Brahmin family whose son was getting his PhD in America. They envisioned us being a perfect match and having a long, happy life together. Everything seemed to be in place.

My family had a lot of love to offer to their new soon-to-be son-in-law, who seemed to be very happy about marrying me. To them, this indicated it wouldn't be just an arranged marriage between Brahmin families, but also about two people who were happy to be getting married to each other. I, on the other hand, was happy to be fulfilling my duty to my family, but I was also apprehensive about marrying someone who was a total stranger.

Before I knew it, my parents and my husband's family had approved of the two of us getting married. Our wedding happened very quickly after that, with all the customary Brahmin rituals and ceremonies, not long after we first met. It was beautiful. I remember how happy everyone was for us, singing and dancing and praying for longevity together. I was terrified. It's traditional for the bride to move into her in-law's home immediately after the wedding, but since my husband was doing his PhD at the University of Illinois, I would be moving not across town, but to the other side of the world.

I needed to have my VISA and papers in place before I could move to America to be with him. Eight months passed by the time everything was in place and before I could move to Illinois to be with my husband. I grew closer to my parents in the time before I left but knew that I would eventually be saying goodbye. When it was finally time to leave, I left a lot of things behind: happy memories, family bonds, friendships. I had no idea what to expect from this new life or where this new adventure might take me.

My flight was a very long one, like most international flights, and on March 18, 1988, my flight landed in America. As soon as I stepped off the plane, life felt different. There was noise, but it was a different kind of noise. Not as overwhleming. The smells were unfamiliar, and I felt like a bit alien in my new surroundings. My husband was there at the Chicago International airport to pick me up and I was elated to see him, but also nervous. We hadn't spent that much time together and now we were going to be sharing a home and a life together.

The two-hour drive to Urbana-Champaign that same night gave us the opportunity to talk, but I was exhausted from my long flight and with the anticipation of what my new home looked like. My husband was attending school and lived in a small apartment right across from campus. I don't know what I expected, but I found that even though the apartment was small, it was still cozy. I could see the university right across the street, lit up and welcoming.

The next morning when I woke up, everything felt so strange and so different. Everything in my surroundings was so completely new, including the cold weather in the middle of March. When I left India it had been hot, but here, I knew I would need new clothes and time to adjust to the temperature. My husband cooked a nice breakfast to make me feel at home and we went out and took care of some necessary paperwork relating to my moving to America. We drove around the city for a while to get a feel of what was going to be my new home. He showed me around the Twin City, which is mostly a college town since the University of Illinois has a huge student body. Pretty much everything there was related to students and the university.

I was amazed by the layout of the area. Illinois is in the heart of the Midwest, which is known as the "Breadbasket of the Nation." It is completely flat and very spread out. It was nothing like the home I had left back in Bihar. And while I adjusted to the space, I had a hard time adjusting to the cold. Not long after I arrived, I experienced my first snow. It would not only form a slippery blanket on the streets and the highways, but it would also crystallize on the branches of all the trees making it look like small droplets of diamonds hanging from them. It was an incredibly beautiful sight to wake up to.

In our time there, I was always amazed by the colors created by the trees lining the Midwest streets in the fall or the first snow of the season that I got to see right from my bedroom window. I hadn't seen anything quite this spectacular in nature ever before. Lines after lines of trees as far as my eyes could see with crystals hanging from it like an amazing phenomenon of physics right in front of me; one of the most breathtaking views I had ever seen. But it had its downside too. The branches would get so heavy with the weight of water and ice that they would break off after a while, resulting in property damage and power outages. This happened the very first year I was there and the intensity of it scared me.

While I was becoming acclimated, my husband and I would spend time in American environments outside, either on campus or some other place together, and go on long drives. The idea was to get familiar with all our American surroundings while we got familiar with each other, too. We were still strangers, trying to understand each other's habits, likes, and dislikes. It could be overwhelming navigating a new language, new culture, and new relationship, but with his guidance and help, I eased into it more and more. There was so much to see and do and so much to learn.

Once my jet lag ended, my new life started in earnest. In the first few days, my husband took care of everything and of me, and patiently taught how things are done in America.

Now it was my turn to do the grown-up thing and take care of him. It still felt like we were "playing house" in many ways, but I slowly started taking on some responsibilities as a wife. I started by doing a little bit of Indian cooking since my husband was very fond of Indian food. It made him happy the way I would go collect books and recipes from the library and make nice Indian dishes for him. He had been single for a long time because he had been so busy with school and absolutely loved that I took time to make all of his favorite meals.

As the months moved from March to April to June, I started to get homesick. The meals I made reminded me of home and I missed everything there, especially my family. I had never been so far away from them. Even the university I had attended in Bihar was right in my hometown and had not required my moving away. I was struggling to understand the woman I was becoming in this new place without my family to ground me.

Being so far away also had its advantages, and I soon realized that even though both my husband and I missed our families, it was ultimately a blessing. In the Indian culture when you marry, you are also married to each other's family. There can be a lot of interference from family members, usually with no apologies made. Arguments inevitably happen in practically all arranged marriages where family involvement is a major part of the marriage. Without that influence, my husband and I got a chance to grow closer together as a married couple, fostering strong love and a stronger relationship in that crucial first year of our marriage. It gave us an opportunity to bond as two individuals, not only growing together in marriage with room to be ourselves but to love each other and to care for each other the way two married people are meant to. We had nobody but

After a while, we trusted each other as friends, and eventually as the soulmates we had become, without our even being aware of it.

each other, and a piece of paper stating we were together in marriage, both in the eyes of God as well as the legal system. We both knew that no matter how much we fought and no matter how tough things got, we had to come back to each other.

After a while, we trusted each other as friends, and eventually as the soulmates we had become, without our even being aware of it. Slowly, we began to fall in love with each other. After about six months or so, we realized how much we had come to depend on each other for our happiness and how much we had become each other's world, as is usually the case when two people end up being each other's world completely. There was no Hindu community where we were, so we spent all of our time together, wrapped up in one another. By the end of the first year of our marriage, we knew for sure that we liked having each other in our lives and loved coming home to each other.

~

Now here we are, about thirty-two years later. I find myself all alone thinking once again about life and what it is all about. As we all know, life can be very unpredictable and has a mind of its own. No matter how much we try to protect ourselves from getting hurt, no matter how much we play safe, no matter how much we plan, no matter how much we prepare ourselves for that rainy day, sometimes the umbrella just isn't big enough.

You remind me I have you and the love we share
The way it feels when I see your sweet face and hold you
Like I have my best friend and my soul I can bare
With you in my life everything seems to fall in place
And this world feels like a beautiful affair

Excerpt from "Way I Feel About You," page 92

Chapter Two

Meaningless over Meaningful

WHILE WE WERE at Urbana Champaign, we struggled. My husband was suffering from a very severe case of burnout and it was taking its toll on his schoolwork, making it very difficult for him to finish his PhD. He also couldn't find a job where he could take a break from his studies and come back and finish his PhD later. He was very unhappy and depressed, and it was affecting our relationship and our marriage. Around that same time, I had made the decision to go back to school and do my undergraduate studies in chemical engineering. I graduated a little later and we moved to the West Coast in California, to the San Francisco Bay area. We hoped that a change of scenery might bring us back together again the same way it had in our early days of marriage.

We got hired in very demanding jobs at the same company. Gone were the long drives and getting-to-know you talks where we could explore. He was a software engineer, and I was a process development engineer working on a next generation tool that was supposed to be a breakthrough from the process end of our industry; the next cutting edge technology tool to be introduced to the marketplace. It was a very stressful and high-pressure job environment.

I was already thirty-five years old, and even though it was demanding, I enjoyed my job. However, I knew that my biological clock was ticking, and there was a lot of pressure from both sides of our families to start a family of our own. My siblings were in that same phase in life of starting a family and I was very excited about the way things were coming together. The buzz of grandkids from every corner brought our entire family closer. My brother is two years younger than me and had a three-month-old son by this time, and my younger sister and her husband, who were newlyweds, were trying to have a family, too. Eventually, they had a son about a year down the road and another one about three years later. I had hoped to be going through all of these changes with them.

While the idea of starting a family and working in the same place should have meant more time spent with each other, it ended up driving us apart. Our individual spaces were being completely dominated by each other's physical presence. It seemed we could never have our own time or space outside of each other at work or at home. We were both stressed and couldn't find any way to find comfort in each other. I also couldn't confide in my family, because I didn't want the unhappiness of my personal life or my marriage woes to be part of their new joy. My husband and I had had this kind of problem before in Illinois but had gone back to being together and then having a happy marriage. I was confident we could work through it again without involving our families or the added expectations from them to make it work.

But our marriage went from bad to worse. Nothing helped, and I knew raising a family in a house where we couldn't agree on anything would be a disaster. We fought constantly. Each fight seemed worse than the last. Eventually our families found out how bad it was and there were several attempts by family and friends to reconcile us. My husband and I would meet and talk and try to communicate with each other, but it turned out to be a futile exercise and wasted effort. Our once loving relationship had slowly burned into intense hate.

After years of this and feeling like we weren't getting anywhere, I decided to return to India and be with my family. They warned me that it was not the right decision to make, but certain mistakes you realize, in hindsight, are meant to be serious regrets. I never could have expected or anticipated just how serious, despite the telltale signs and sage advice given to me. I had to see it all play out for myself.

I had been gone for fifteen years from India. When I got married it was like a separation from my parents had happened, too. There were things I could not go back to. In India, I found out that what I used to call my family had stopped being my family a long time ago. At a time when I needed them most because of the turmoil that was going on in my life, I realized that my family was embarrassed that their daughter was back home and going through a divorce. Divorce was unheard of in our Brahmin families and communities. It is a huge sacrilege there and plenty in the community won't have anything to do with you or your family after a divorce has occurred. Because arranged marriages are the norm in these communities, there is pressure to make sure divorce remains unacceptable from a religious and societal point of view. Families with divorcees are treated as outcasts

> I had returned home for support but ended up being more alone and isolated than ever.

in terms of any kind of social or future family ties—like a new marriage—with that family.

My parents did not like having that kind of shame brought home to them. They tried very hard to talk me out of my divorce, but my marriage was already over. In their attempt to talk me out of it, the proceedings dragged on for a period of four years before it was finally granted by the court system in India.

I had nowhere to turn without their support. The people I had grown up with, people who used to be my friends, had all moved out and were scattered all over India, were married with children, and had busy lives of their own. My parents were close to retirement and my dad retired from his job a few months after I had moved back. After his retirement, he opened a consultancy firm in his area of expertise since he was a nationally renowned technologist and a scholar. I got involved in working for him as much as possible and avoided the social environment completely since it was an extremely uncomfortable situation and exceedingly difficult to deal with people's prejudice and hatred. I had returned home for support but ended up being more alone and isolated than ever.

Things continued like this for a few years. I tried to stay focused on work while also trying to accept my new environment and move on with my life. But the embarrassment of having a divorced daughter was too much for my dad to deal with. The stress resulted in his failing health and eventually his death in November of 2011. After he died, my family environment became even more strained. My mom and my brother did not like having me as part of the family and blamed me for my father's early demise. Eventually, I was cast out of the one place I felt I had belonged all those years ago.

After my divorce and my father's death, I realized that I'd not only lost my husband, I had also lost my identity as an Indian woman. It was not just about wanting to be accepted by my Brahmin community because of my divorce, but also about the fact that what I used to identify with very strongly were the people and community I loved. These people had defined me as much as my religion, my roots, and my ancestry. All the close relationships in my life were all Indians—from my husband to my family members to friends coming from the same Brahmin community. I had never made friends easily in America because I was still so tied to my roots and my job took up most of my time. Once the divorce was finalized, it was equivalent to losing my Indian identity completely. I had failed in my role as an Indian woman; to be a homemaker and a mother. I was rejected. I had never imagined that people and relationships that once gave meaning to my life and defined my happiness would shun me.

∼

When my falling out with my family first happened, it felt like my world was falling apart. There were times it was very difficult to get myself out of it and very difficult to console myself about the loss I was going through. It would be at those exact moments where I would also be reminded of the importance of moving on; that life is not just about breathing, existing, but also about living fully and in a meaningful way.

Who until yesterday
Had meant more to me than life itself
Today it's like looking in the mirror
At the face of a stranger

Excerpt from "These Words That Still Haunt Me from the Past," page 45

Chapter Three

Life is a Stranger

ITH MY FAMILY breaking down in India, I soon realized it was time to move on and I made the decision to return to the US. I tried looking for a job, but it was very difficult to find one because of the long hiatus I had taken from the American job market. I had been gone for seven years. I was older. I was foreign. I had extensive experience, but I just wasn't the best candidate. It seemed like a good idea to go back to school and get my master's degree in chemical engineering since my undergraduate degree was from one of top of the chemical engineering schools in the field. I applied to a couple of schools and got a response from the University of South Florida in their master's program.

When I returned to school, I realized that it wasn't just the job market that wasn't fond of my age. Being older, it's difficult to fit into the school environment—or for that matter, plenty of other environments where everybody is either half your age or twice your age. It was just like being back home in India, where nearly everybody was my parent's generation and my parent's age. Once again, I had that feeling of being displaced, leading to feelings of abandonment and suffering. Everything in the universe seemed to be in place and yet I didn't fit in. I always seem to be at the wrong place at the wrong time.

It was the beginning of the fall semester at my university, and I was returning from school to my apartment on a beautiful day. I was walking home, enjoying the breeze on my face, thinking about how I was adjusting to life as a student again. Just when I was about to cross the street, a car came out of nowhere and hit me right in front of my apartment building. I tried to keep my balance to stop myself from falling as the car hit me, but the car kept moving. As I completely lost my balance and came crashing down, I realized this was going to be a serious fall. The pain was intense and everywhere. The thought of death crossed my mind. I wasn't sure that I would come out of this alive.

Everything happened so quickly. Within a matter of a few seconds, it went from being an ordinary day to realizing that the very last thought I'm probably going to have is about my own death. It felt like I laid there for hours, struggling not to move, but thankfully another car that was passing by stopped at the scene. A young woman got out of the car and immediately called 911. She tried to help me stand, but I couldn't move at all. I remember looking up at the clouds and hearing the noise of the ambulance and police sirens and praying I was going to survive. The paramedics carefully put me on the gurney, and I was rushed to the emergency room of a nearby hospital. The doctors immediately took tests and scans and found out that I had serious fractures in the bones of both my elbows and my knees. I needed immediate and complicated surgery. Having them hover over me in chaos, aching with pain and fear, was one of the scariest moments in my life.

The rest of it after that is, as they say, history. I was in the hospital and rehabilitation for several months, which led to a disruption in my studies. I had complications from the surgeries and required a wheelchair for six months. It took me a long time to walk again because any kind of physical activity would lead to pain and severe exhaustion. Climbing stairs, even getting ordinary chores done became an arduous task. As a result, I had to make the decision to take even more time off from school.

I was also in a huge financial mess because the insurance company of the person driving the car that hit me didn't cover all the hospital bills resulting from the accident, nor did my graduate school insurance (which covers only the most basic injuries and ailments like most graduate school insurance does). As a result of health problems stemming from my accident, I found myself without a job, without money, all alone, and homeless at an age where most people are well settled in life and seriously considering retirement.

Breathing was the only meaning left.

Not long after that, I ended up at the homeless shelter run by the Catholic diocese. For a long, long time after I found myself still reeling from what had happened on that fateful day. It was becoming difficult to figure out where to go from there or how to move into the next phase of my life. I had already had difficulty finding a job because of my age, my immigrant status, the gap in my resume, and now it was even more complicated because of my health problems. Depression set in. My life seemed to be in complete shambles. Everything I had worked so hard for—like putting myself through school, to do something I loved to do like working in technology—seemed to have all gone down the drain. Everyday life seemed like a chore. Breathing was the only meaning left.

In the midst of my recovery and trying to settle in at the shelter, I became a target. As a foreigner I have to be careful to stay away from addicts. Everyone in the homeless shelter is displaced, which often leads to anger that is then exacerbated by drugs and alcohol. One day I got attacked in the dining hall.

It was broad daylight, and I was minding my own business, when someone approached me who had threatened me before. Without warning, they assaulted me in front of everybody in the room. I had just recovered from the car accident, and now my hand was broken. I was in a cast for about eight weeks leaving me unable to do chores or daily tasks that I had been helping with. I was living in fear of the people around me instead of having a safe and secure place of my own.

As I seemed to be getting further and further into anxiety and depression, I realized that I would have to do something drastic about pulling myself out of it. Somewhere I had read that you have basically two choices in life: One is to choose to be happy, the other is to let life get the better of you and be miserable and depressed. In order to choose happiness, I knew that I would have to make a concerted effort to get out of my depression and take those first few tiny steps to make a conscious decision to choose to be happy. I then immediately made the decision to do a few things differently.

I knew I was smarter than my problems. I decided to come up with a plan of what I felt I needed to do in order to change my homelessness status quo. I sat down with a pen and paper—like I often do when something is bothering me—and decided to write down some of my emotions and turmoil and then take an approach towards resolving them. I knew I needed to give my life a new purpose and direction since nothing had turned out the way I thought it might. I came up with my own ten-step program, so to speak, so that I could move on the way I wanted and needed to. The following was the plan that I put together as a solemn promise I made to myself to change forever for the better:

- Find a job and do what I love to do best, playing in technology where I get to push the limits of my intelligence.
- Have an incredibly nice place of my own that I always wanted that I can call home.

- ☺ Give my life new purpose by learning to leave my baggage behind and give it a new direction.
- ☺ Find happiness again and give my life a new meaning.
- ☺ Learn to love myself again knowing that even when there is no one, God is always there.
- ☺ Know the importance of being kind to yourself and to others.
- ☺ Always believe in yourself because it gives you the strength and courage to do something beautiful in life.
- ☺ Realize the importance of being involved because this world can be a cruel place.
- ☺ Follow my passions in life and in things I strongly believe in, like being a victim's rights advocate, a cause that is close to my heart.
- ☺ Never ever stop dreaming because that alone gives you a purpose and direction in life to do something meaningful.

I had a dream. I had a plan. I had a purpose. I enjoyed writing down all of my thoughts and moving through the emotions there. It was healing. Since the job search wasn't taking me anywhere, I decided to give my writing and poems more serious consideration. I have a strong passion for writing about the tragedies that some of us experience, and I decided to put more time and effort into that endeavor.

I did something outside of my comfort zone and shared some of my poems with the people at the shelter as well as with various church groups that came in to volunteer. I got several compliments and my self-confidence in my writing grew. Quite a few people asked me for my permission to post them on the board at their church since they were very inspiring and motivating. I decided to submit a few for review and possible publication to a few publishing companies. I got a couple of serious inquiries. Taking the leap and putting myself out there was the biggest challenge, and even if I wasn't compensated, I knew that I would be elated just to have my name out there.

$$\sim$$

Filled with enthusiasm for this new direction, I have tried to incorporate healthy habits like staying positive about the future, making a few friends that I'd had a little bit of conversation with instead of keeping completely to myself, doing at least twenty hours of volunteer work, and even though I didn't have any income, going to the beach once in a while and trying to relax. I don't know what this next phase of my life is preparing me for, but I am determined to enjoy every moment of it.

This life that is sometimes a story of pain and sorrow
This life that is sometimes a story of love and sweetness and tomorrow
One thing though will always stay
You neither can quit nor run away

Excerpt from "When it Comes to Life," page 112

Chapter Four

Never Giving Up – Having Faith

A FEW YEARS AGO, when it felt like I was literally losing my religion, and everything that possibly could go wrong did go wrong, like some Murphy's law of the universe that had set itself in motion, I found myself asking this very important question: *What is the meaning of life and what is this life about anyway?* How do I come to terms with the hurt inflicted on me by others? How do I come to terms with this treachery that I felt? How do I make the wounds go away? How do I heal, and make the scars soften? How do I give my life a new meaning and a new direction so that I am then able to move on?

In asking myself these questions and writing on them for this chapter, I realized that the most important relationship we have in life is our relationship with God. I personally believe that this one relationship dictates the rest of our relationships in life, which then tangibly translates into personal happiness for most of us. God helps us stay sane in this insane world, which, for some of us, includes abandonment from family and friends to loss of loved ones, to even homelessness. The trauma that you go through, and the panicking that you then feel inside that just won't stop, is one of the worst feelings in life. When that happens, we are able to deal with it better when we have a sincere and close relationship with ourselves, and with God. This gives us the hope to move forward and come out of our tough times in one piece, and a little stronger.

I also realize that this relationship we have with God should not always be in the form of just going to the church or the temple. I didn't have the opportunity to attend a Hindu temple in Illinois or California, but God was always with me. I don't need the physical building to feel His presence. Because of my exposure to various faiths and religions in my life, I feel like I have a "melting pot" view when it comes to religion and how I see God. I'm fortunate that the times I feel I can cultivate my relationship with Him the most are when I'm actively being involved with things like volunteer work, where I'm helping other people. It not only makes a difference in someone else's life, but also in our own lives and can have a very healing effect on our own trauma. Knowing that the pain and suffering was not all in vain if we can help others through that experience, helps us feel better about what did happen to us when it comes to making our peace with it; that maybe it was God having an important conversation with us so that we could go on and be that voice of change.

After I became estranged from my family, I realized the importance of not dwelling on the past but leaving my baggage behind. That, to me, defined living again. Now I know that no matter where I am in life or where it takes me, I can always face issues head-on instead of allowing them to bring me down. Whenever I am at the crossroads, where it feels like life is throwing me those tough decisions, I try to make a conscious decision not to run away. No matter what, I can live fearlessly, unafraid of the future, because God is always there, and I have faith in my ability to overcome.

I also realized how important it is, as someone who has been through this kind of traumatic experience of family abandonment, to make sure that this does not happen to another human being again. I made a pact with myself to be part of a voice for people like me. To actually do something about it and help prevent another person from getting hurt in the same way. I have had to make my peace with life in many situations. I keep my faith and then move on with this renewed promise that I make to myself, of not allowing my past to cripple me ever again and I hope I can help others choose the same path.

With as much as I've been through, I have also seen and experienced the kindness of strangers. They have been my light in the darkness. They have shown me that even fleeting relationships can have more of an impact on us when framed with kindness than even family bonds can. But when you have seen life like this, then you know that even finding love again is not the complete answer. Love doesn't provide permanency or meaning to your life. I have found that people would come and go and that love may not last forever. And that's okay. Friends and family move out of your life, but sometimes strangers can give love more beautifully than any family ever could; something that not even your wildest imagination had prepared you for. If I had not accepted this reality, I would once again be constantly finding myself having to define and redefine happiness. Instead, it is important to define happiness as the relationships we have with ourselves first. In this way, I do not let someone else define it exclusively for me, and I can appreciate the lessons these people have for me and move on.

Reflecting on the relationships I've had, the many friends, strangers, and teachers, makes me realize that nobody in this world escapes tragedy or suffering. That this life is a journey. It will always remain a journey and there will never be any easy answers or easy solutions to life's complex problems that get hurled our way. It spares no one, no matter who or what you are. No matter how much you try to run away from it or try to protect yourself from getting hurt, life, being life, will always have a mind of its own. It dictates its own terms as the ups and downs that we all have to live through, along with all the meandering roads in between.

Life, you realize, is not just about the happiness you can grab once in a while as it passed you by. It is always about relationships you form and foster with friends and family. It is our work, our passions, as well as our other pursuits, that define us as individuals. Some things in life money will never be able to buy. We have to build it with a lot of love, as something we invest in life, as our personal happiness and happiness of people that come into our lives through God's guidance. We can build a solid foundation of love, trust, faith, and relationships as important pillars, on which all our happiness lay, that constitute our support system. They keep our world from falling apart when, for whatever reason, tragedy strikes. In this way our happiness is firmly in place, like a well-tended plant that flourishes into a beautiful fully grown tree. This is like taking an approach to attacking the complexities of life and how it gets defined, by making sure that all the important elements of happiness in our lives are firmly in place. This kind of approach to dealing with life helps us heal. You are then able to pick up the pieces and move on with your life a little less broken and a little less worse for the wear.

Maybe what it really takes is not just about the success and achievements or the materialistic things we have acquired

> Beautiful paths may not necessarily be a bed of roses in the short term, but in the long term they have a beautiful view.

in life, but also a combination of giving and receiving as in relationships, along with some of the important things we say and do in life as individuals. It then encompasses both our physical, as well as our emotional needs, thereby addressing all our needs and requirements at all levels. When it is a combination of all of these things, like success, achievements, relationships, giving, and involvement, are we then able to achieve that higher level of happiness where we are meant to be, instead of someone who just breathes and goes through the motions of life as I once did. It makes us push our limits and achieve that higher level and higher platform of achieving the unthinkable that only the human brain is capable of doing. This expansion of humanity gives us a better life and a fair and kind society, of which we all can then be proud citizens.

True happiness as we all know comes from beautiful thoughts, words and deeds, and the paths we take in life. These paths that determine the environment and the people that end up in our lives, becoming part of our lives. Our thoughts and words determine the paths we choose to take. Beautiful paths may not necessarily be a bed of roses in the short term, but in the long term they have a beautiful view. When you take a beautiful path, you meet beautiful people along the way. You make bonds and relationships that you can see and cherish forever in your life. Like roses, we know they may not last forever, but they will always bloom again.

When you are having these conversations with life, it is important to realize how important it is to never ever stop believing in yourself. Life is meant to be lived with a few regrets, because they will inevitably happen along the way—that will always be a part of life. But the few tragic events of your life should not singlehandedly define all of your happiness, or your identity, and should not be allowed to define all of your future happiness. Life is about taking on challenges and facing it head on and living it the only way it's meant to be lived: fearlessly. After all, who has seen tomorrow?

Author's Note

With that in mind, I'd like to provide a brief introduction to the poems on the following pages. You have now read my journey of how I got to be where I am today and what has shaped and molded me. Maybe I will always be a misfit. Maybe I was never meant to fit into any one place in time, but I hope that through my poetry, I can provide hope to those of you that need it, and a voice to those who feel silenced.

Part Two

Poems

Poems of Hope

Ashes of Love Left Behind
(As I Move on with My Life)

It was a cold winter night
Miles and miles of snow and ice
Eerie silence like a deafening noise
Not a single soul in sight
I could feel the chill in my bones
Everything lost and long away from home
What used to be the castle of my relationships of love
All turned out to be lies and this cold dense fog
And just ashes now left behind
Of what used to be my life
And full of hurt and pain inside
And things I no longer can call mine
Like hell hath no fury
On this cold lonely winter night

Far away from home I could see a glimmer of light
Coming from a bonfire burning far away in sight
As I got closer I could see
Another lonely soul just like me
His soul hurting just like mine
Reminding me of a familiar face from some other time
Like he had also lost everything in this world
I wondered to myself
What brought him here
To this God forsaken place tonight
Not meant for a soul to wander
On this cold winter night
Was it something like my story
Of life just happening
Where every person of your life
Turned out to be the same old story
All it took was one single spark to ignite
And your world that came crumbling apart
And all your meaningful relationships
And all your hard work gone in one single night
Why is it something when it feels so right
Not meant to last
Is it previous karma or just distant past

And then you wonder once again
What is it about love and life
That you desperately want to hold on to something tight
As I moved closer towards him I wondered
What was it that drew me to him
What was this pull that I had towards this stranger
Like I have known him for a long time this lone ranger
All alone just like me in this lonely night
Like two strangers
Who have known each other
For a very long time
Or maybe all our lives
Or maybe it was just about two lost souls
Lost in this lonely crowd called life
Who have lost everything in this world
Not even a shoulder to lean on or cry
Desperately trying to make sense of this cruel world

Just then he looked up at me and smiled
I was lost forever in his eyes
I realized he was a familiar face from my past
Long time ago of love lost
We had once known each other
And had gone our separate ways
Here we are once again
After all these years
It's like life telling you it had come to a full circle
And once again life had thrown us together
Into each other's arms forever like two strangers
Who had got lost in this bustling world
In this confusing journey called life
Somewhere along the way who had lost their way
Two people who had always belonged together
Two people who were always meant for each other
Meant to kiss each other's pain away

Feet in Shackles and Slavery

God sometimes this world feels like a prison
Feet in shackles and like slavery
Hands tied and tears you cannot hide
Time you cannot turn back
God love lost and wounds that will not heal
And blood that bleeds and you have become numb to the pain
God chains of bondage like a noose
Around my throat making it hard to breathe
Like a rope hanging from a tree
And your listless body that no longer weeps
God tears that roll down my eyes it's like life is in a quagmire
And it feels like long before I came on this earth
This story had already been written for me
Like a death sentence you were born with
That you just cannot escape
The noise is deafening and a shiver runs down my spine
God the angst that I feel so deep within my soul
This inner turmoil within me screaming in agony
Dread keeping me awake at nights
And as I looked in the mirror
I could see the disquiet etched on my face
That I feel at this treachery and betrayal
And once again I woke up filled with trepidation
Cold sweat breaking on my forehead
And my palms all clammy breaking in sweat
No matter how hard I try or where I run away
Once again it feels like this path had been paved for me
Long before I took my first breath in this inhuman race
Reminding me how cruel this world can sometimes be with no escape
Then I close my eyes once again and death feels like a beautiful escape
Then in the distant I hear the church bell ringing and I realize
That it is not always about your religion but about other people's religion as well
When you are bleeding and this life makes absolutely no sense
And you are at the crossroads of your life and all lost in confusion
God then you remind me that when one door closes another opens
God wanted us to smile and that is why we breathe and that is the reason

This Life is Nothing but a Journey

You don't get to go back and correct your mistakes
In this life somethings you just cannot change
Don't keep looking back
What's done is done
Don't look back
Because past cannot be undone
Life stops for nobody
Whether we are somebody or nobody
Moving on is another name of life
In this life that's to stay
Moving on is the game of life
We all have to play
No matter how hard we try to run away
We are all out here in this journey called life
Arms wide open head held high
The world ahead of us
An endless field and open skies
Future unknown and nothing we can take for granted
Not even our closest ties
Our destinations in life are numerous
With many crossroads in between
Only God knows where this journey is going to take us
Oblivious as we are of our destiny
Life stops for nobody
It is like a river that runs deep
And keeps moving forward
Likewise we have to keep moving forward
In this journey of life it stops for nobody
If you sit on the sidelines too long
For someone to come along
Waiting for the tide to subside
Instead of taking life by the horns
Life will pass you by
Without love by your side
You will never be able to reach your destination
You have only one life
Why live life with resignation
Always moving forward is the sign of life
Always moving forward
Is another game of life
And stagnation is the sign of death

These Words That Still Haunt Me from the Past

These words that haunt me from the past
That reminds me of the religion that was
Stops me from moving on the way I need to
To put behind me the things I should
You the embodiment of hate
I desperately holding on to the past
Your mind all made up
The way you were wronged
My world falling apart and all torn
In which universe should things be so wrong
You meant to me embodiment of love itself
With you it was still about embarrassment and regrets
This hatred you felt
Things no longer the same
My world that is falling apart
My belief system that could not believe
Love could have such an ugly face
Now that I know how much you hated
Now that I know what you meant
The religion of hatred you were
My world of love that you had always been
The strangers we turned out to be in this life
This religious moment of my life
This catastrophe that has befallen
Who until yesterday
Had meant more to me than life itself
Today it's like looking in the mirror
At the face of a stranger
Who had it all planned
Losing my religion
My world falling apart
My belief system shaken
Speechless at the loss
That someone I once loved do much
Could hurt me like this and betray my trust
Blood gushing to my head
Anguish I feel inside
Or is it just the pain I feel
That is leaving me all numb inside

I try to shake it away
I try to tell myself it's all a lie
Yet as I see the ashes of what's left behind
Says the story of what happened tonight
Tears that just won't stop
As it rolls down my eyes
Feeling sorry for myself
Even there cannot escape or hide
No matter how many tears I shed
Desperately trying to wipe them away
Still cannot console my broken heart
Which weeps once again
At this betrayal I feel inside
Still cannot stop this feeling
Of the hurt inside
My world that had fallen apart
Once again trying to make sense of it all
To make the hurt go away
This sense of disbelief
This disquiet I feel
As my heart weeps
Like a cry from my soul
Which is still searching
Trying to make sense of it all
At this loss
And my heart which refuses to heal
As I once again
Try to wipe away the tears
As it silently rolls down my face

Shades of My DNA

Shades of my DNA makeup
That makes me the intelligence
That I am as face of bold
My few shades of grey
The perfection that I am not
That I also happen to be in this world
The weak that I am when it is intelligence dictated
As who I am making a statement about us all
The pretentious that I become
When it is couple of religions I try to keep
Despite life and all of it's calls
The paths I do take in life and the ones I don't
As who I am that does get defined for us all
Like a winter blizzard day in November
Life that still happened with a vengeance
Like a final curtain call
Life in its cruelest shape
As unjustified vengeance of a maniacs rage
Where life had come to a stall
You try to distance yourself from it
Yet it becomes an arduous task to escape like closing walls
I cry a few tears for myself
Then I think of him who created us all
The gamut of emotions running through my head
As to how human life and human dignity
Can be this priceless call
Trying to make sense of it all in this moment of truth
This conversation that I have with him who always stands tall
All alone in this forsaken place
Where nothing in this world no longer makes any sense at all
As I think of him I then realize
He does exist and wipe away my tears as they fall
With this knowledge that he still loves me
I try to make my peace with it at this unthinkable gall
With this truth that he still cares for me
I try to leave my baggage behind after this ravaging Mistral
Finally leaving that winter blizzard day behind me
I then proudly move on with a resolution
Never to look back at it no matter what

With this new purpose to make a difference in my own life
And in another person's life
Where this does not happen to another human being
This inhuman appall
To make our hearts heal when soul is hurting
So that another soul does not get lost in the crowd
Where life had come to a crawl
To be able to touch another person's life
To be each other's happiness and strength
When life's darkest moment feels like a never ending nightfall
With this renewed passion to be that change in my own life
And in another person's life
I proudly move on as I think of him who created us all

Life is Such a Mystery
(Looking Back at Life; My Conversations with God)

Life I have known you for a long time now
You are still a mystery
Life I have known you for a long time now
You still puzzle me
When I was young and invincible
I thought I could conquer you
I am older and wiser now
And yet here I am still trying to make sense of you
I still cannot recognize your footprints
Life, why are you so scary and uncertain?
Life I have known you for a long time now
I still do not understand you
God what were you thinking when you created us
Are we just your mere pawns?
That can easily be broken?
Why do we face heartbreak?
Why is pain and sorrow a part of our life?
When you have the resource of the universe
At your disposal when you are creating us
Why is so much sorrow and pain a part of us
You can create incredible beauty as something beautiful we see all around us
Then why is there so much misery in this world?

You tell us happiness is the way of life
Which we all chase after as what we know how it is supposed be as the
ultimate meaning of life
Then why is it such a fleeting thing?
Why does it not last?
Why is It so transient
Why can't we capture it the way happiness is supposed to be and make it ours forever
Why do you feel we need to know sorrow?
That too quite like this in order to recognize life
Why can't happiness be a permanent companion
As in you and I and something beautiful we do in life
Life I have known you for a long time now
Why are you still such a mystery
God why is this life such a tough journey
The paths we take filled with so much uncertainty

Why can't we have little more guarantees in life
Especially when it comes to people who come into our lives
Why should the future be such a huge question mark?
Do give us some clue about the paths
Just like the clouds in the sky warn us about the rainfall
The lightening before the thunderstorm
About the storm
God give us some clue about our destination
So that life does not scare us this way about our future
God why is loss a part of our life?
Why is loss an inevitable thing?
If loss is supposed to be part of our life
Then why do you put people in our lives in the first place
Why do you make us care?
Why do you give us attachment?
Why do you make us fall in love?
Why do you give us these feelings
Where we cannot let go?
And get very badly hurt?
Feelings that make loss so unbearable
Feelings that make us hurt like this
Wounds that won't heal
And scars that still remain
God these questions that comes to my mind always about you and I and why
is it this way

God why is love is quite like this
Why is it such an elusive thing
Why make it an important part of our destiny and journey?
When it causes so much hurt and pain?
Why does it sometimes feel like we were meant to meet?
When often people go their separate ways
If people are destined to be each other's happiness?
Why not make it feel like love that lasts all the way?
As something forever as love is meant to be?
Why is something that can be a source of so much happiness
Causes so much hurt and pain?
God what kind of world is this?
Where loss is the ultimate thing from above?
What kind of life is this where people in this world are so inhuman?

Alone in this Crowd Called Life

When life feels meaningless
And another day gone by
And I feel like I am losing my religion
And no shoulder to lean on or cry
Just another person
That's lost in the crowd
As life passes me by
It's then I pick up the pieces
And take on something new
With a new paintbrush
To paint the canvas
Which until yesterday was a little too blue
With new shades and hues
Making sure I always keep my faith
And stay close to my roots
(I know it has been long time due
Time to move on my heart says and knew)
To give my life new meaning
And a meaningful view

When I am feeling lonely
And all lost and sad
Then I look at the deep blue sea
In front of me
And where it meets the deep blue skies
And the lines blur
And my eyes well up with tears
Is it all my imagination
That life sometimes feels so hopeless
That I just want to cry
It's then I go to my favorite spot
That I always go to
When I am feeling sad
Once again I look at the deep blue sea
In front of me
And then I don't feel so bad

When I Am Feeling the Blues

When I am feeling the blues
And everything around me
Feels unglued
And I am all lost and confused
And I have no idea what to do
Everything feels like a mess
And I do not have a clue
It's then
I curl up on my couch in front of my TV
In my favorite pajamas
With my favorite brew
And my favorite coffee mug on cue
And hot chocolate to comfort me
And to my rescue
To heal my soul
Which feels like a battered bruise
And watch reruns of X files and its crew
And everything feels much better
And brand new
And they chase away my blues

When life feels hopeless
And everything lost
Every ties of your life
Feels like it was a serious knot
Heavy price you paid for love
And at what cost
It's then I sit on my porch
And listen to my favorite music
And reflect on the march
Sounds from the past
No longer playing a trick
And my head feels clearer
And feelings resolved
About my ordeal
My wounds heal
And I pick up the pieces
And move forward
With a new zeal

And my spirits soar
And then once again
Get back into life with a roar

When life feels frustrating
And everything seems wrong
All laws of physics
Seems like Murphy's law
Every path I take
Turns out to be a dead end instead
To a journey unknown
And path I still had to tread
And I am at the crossroads of my life
And I don't know which way to go
For my bruised soul to survive
It's then I go on a long drive
To my favorite city
Where everything about it
Is breathtaking beauty
I take a deep breath
And for a moment I lose myself
In God's awesome creation in front of me
And I think to myself
The person who created this
Must have something good planned for me too

Far Away from Home
(As I Try to Leave My Baggage Behind Where Life Feels Like It Has Come to a Standstill)

Far away from home
Once again lost and confused
Trying to get over my wounds
Entangled in the same old moves
Every name different again
Every face still feels the same
Same old games
Heart that profusely bleeds
Reasons I give to myself to make my peace
Life that brings me down
Love that I can no longer call mine
Relationship that I once had with them was just in my head
Everyone else that has moved on
Things that you cannot go back to no matter what
Long time ago without my knowing
All the rules that had changed completely
This face that has a sweet smile
Yet you can see past it and feel the hatred
You try to move on but it refuses to go away
Despite your best efforts it lingers on and continues to stay
You then realize what life is trying to say
Leaving me in no doubt for me to stay lost or confused or to take it any other way
Then you realize then that at the age of twenty one when I got married
I also did get my emotional emancipation in actuality from all my family that day
No longer any ties to hold it together
My world that got fiercely defined today
It was only I who was still holding on to the past
Unaware of what had been the reality of my life for a long time now
Just when it feels like all is lost and nowhere to escape
Life once again reminds me to stop dwelling on the loss or the March past
But to move on because life still goes on
Because what you know now has been the reality of your life for a long time now
Now that I know for sure
Knowing fully well that I cannot go back no matter what
Decision then made that this path I will never tread again
A promise I then make to myself of protecting myself so that I do not bleed
like this ever again

Where you wish things were still the same
Understanding the importance of distancing myself so that I can heal
Once again I try to pick up the pieces and console myself
What is this game that life plays with us when it comes to love that you are
faced with this kind of loss?
What is it about life that you still want love when it hurts like this?
That you barely come out of it in one piece and just accepting the reality it's
over is the only way to deal with it
As I try to move on I wonder do I just call it life or should I call it something else
Once again with this renewed promise I make to myself that no one can ever
hurt me like this ever again
No longer lost and confused about few things about my life that had felt out
of place now explained
What had defined my world for a long time now all lies
As I move on I wonder why does life sometimes turn out to be this way
You know when you love someone It is not supposed to be like this
Love is not supposed to be hurtful
Love is not supposed to be vindictive or mean
My heart that once again that did break
The hurt that still stays and just won't go away
Everyday I die a little
My life that did not get shattered
My world that did not get turned upside down
My soul that once again sobs a little
Once again I cry for myself a little
As I try to make my peace
As I try to move on

Life is Such a Quagmire

Life can sometimes be such a quagmire
And it sometimes feels like such a satire
Nothing in this world permanent and universe seems to conspire
No matter what may or may not have transpired
Everything seems so quintessential within our reach yet not near
And all the best laid plans that misfire
And dominoes effect that sets into motion that has gone haywire
It's like a Billionaire rubbing our nose in it once again by being on the cover of Esquire
And no more challenges left for them but few countries to acquire
It's like a deer caught in the headlights a price so dear
While I am sitting roasting marshmallows on the bonfire
The unknown all around me sometimes makes me perspire
This life sometimes feels like I am walking on tight wire
And being thrown into eye of the danger without being equipped with right attire
At my wits end trying to make sense of my life and trying to get inspired
Maybe God will send me a sign the skies above me are so sapphire
In this crooked world things to stay clear
And things to stay away from and steer
With this bustling world streets of dire
And hustling strangers such crooked liars
It's like being out of a pan and into a fryer
And it feels like blood is being sucked out of you by a vampire
To this beautiful thought that so cavalier
It's like the beating drums of the town crier
Spelling the death knell on your favorite team that's about to retire

It feels good the weekend is finally here
You get to tell your boss that's for sire
And you are not his slave for hire
And enjoy the weekend to my heart's desire
With a tight kick from my roomie on my rear
It's time to get the engine of my Chevrolet on fire
And feel the rubber burning on the tire
And time to kickback and enjoy life in full gear
With your best friends and cold beer
In high spirits and all around cheer
Having fried clams and crab at the pier
And your girlfriend in short skirts to admire
It's like having on your arms the celebrity Brittney Spears

Making you feel like the man of the year
In this life we all have to endear
To live life to the fullest a rule to live by and to adhere
In God's eyes we should consider this as the final frontier
No matter how the game of life may seem to appear
Ultimately we all have to persevere
Work hard and play hard only compliment you can give to yourself so sincere
Few things in this life you should always revere
Treat this world like a movie with you as the premiere
Reaching the heights and soaring the skies we all aspire
This happens to be life's most beautiful elixir
And it's about sailing the high seas in high speed without fear

Moving on Anyway is Another Name of Life

You are not the only one in this journey of life
People will come and go into your life
Some to stay
And make a difference
Others as passers by
And lessons to be learnt in may day
Some bring happiness into your life
Others are just a lesson to be learnt

Why waste time playing the blame game
And what could or could not have been
Since nothing ever really stays the same
When it's lot simpler to leave the bankruptcies of your life
And just move on
One way or another
They will all leave their mark today
In a known or in an unknowing way
Like footprints in the sand
Affecting your destiny and your mind
No matter which path we take

The path ahead is filled with ups and down
Destiny unknown
And opportunities that will come and go
The path ahead is filled with curve balls
And shortcuts easy to take and stray
It is not always about being right
it is also not always about being wrong
Nor is it easy to stay on the path
When temptations all around us are abound
The path we still take to get to our destination
It still happens to be as important
As the one in our imagination
Because the path we take
Defines who and what we are
The path we do take
Ultimately defines us as the person we are

Change is another name of life
Changing with times is an
Important survival game of life
That we all have to play
Changing with times in this tough world
Gives you a strong hold
To keep moving forward strong and bold
Adapting to changing times
Is important in winning the game of life

You do not get too many chances at winning
No matter how hard you strife
This world belongs to the one
Who changes with time and keeps on ticking
This world belongs to the person
Who keeps on moving forward at all times
The world belongs to the person
Who keeps moving on in life
Hold your head up high and accept change
And keep moving forward
Because that is how you win this game

So Go Out There and Make a Difference

What are you scared of
All you need is courage
Not unheard of
Don't let people stop you or fold
Don't be scared of this world
Don't be scared of what people will say
People will talk no matter what you do have to do or say
Remember it is not always about your religion
But also about theirs and their blatant assumptions
Go out there and make a difference
First and foremost in your own life
And that will give you the strength to do so in other people's life
Obstacles will always be there
That in essence is life
Not a smooth journey no matter how much you prepare
Meant to be removed from your path and overcome
If you don't remove them
How will you get to your destination?
Go conquer this world
This world is yours
Go make a difference
You were born to do so
The day you were born
This world is your playground
Don't let anything stop you
Success is yours to achieve
All you have to do is set your heart to it and believe
You can change the world
So do take the initiative
But also always remember you need to be strong first
Intelligence and power comes with responsibility (in this world)
Let your passion guide you
And allow your imagination to soar
You were meant to do great things
Never ever sell yourself short
Go change this world
It belongs to those who dare
If you have will and determination
You can achieve anything no matter how rare

This world is filled with people who need heroes
Go out there and reach out to them
And give them hope
Give them an opportunity at a better world
And stop people from getting lost in the fold
Go out there and make a difference
In your own life and in other people's life as well
You were meant to do great things
Do not let anything stop you
Believe in yourself
And the world will believe in you
Believe in yourself
Go out there
Make a difference
Believe in yourself
Go out there
Change the world

After all Who Has Seen Tomorrow

Baby who has seen tomorrow
So do borrow
A page of happiness from life
And fill it with all the colors of the rainbow
Baby why be so sad
When this world can be yours
Accept what you cannot control
And make happiness your goal
This life is after all too short a journey
So go live it with no regrets
If there is one lesson we should all takeaway
Life spares no one
And comes everyone's way
A little bit of high
A little bit of low
Sometimes we have no choice
But to go with the flow
This life is after all too short a journey
So go live it with no regrets honey

Baby do not look back too much
This world is also filled with lowlifes and disgusts
After all what is there to gain
Sometimes it is better to move on
Than to dwell on the pain
If it was meant to be
It would not have gone away
What is the point in feeling loss of something
That was never really yours in the first place
Because if it was yours
It would not have gone away
Life is too short a journey
Why live it with regrets anyway
So go out and live life and seize the day

Baby this life is nothing
But a story of pleasure and pain
A little bit of sunshine
And a little bit of rain
A little bit of loss

A little bit of gain
Along with a little bit of hard work
And a little bit of play
A little bit of giving
A little bit of taking
A little bit of singing
And a little bit of mingling
Baby it is all part of life
And it is all here to stay
Baby it is all part of life
And it is all here to stay
After all if you snooze
You will lose
Because life has a mind of its own
And it will keep on ticking
In the end we are all just glad
That we are all alive and still kicking
Life is too short a journey to live with regrets anyway
So go out and live life and seize the day
Always remember
Life is about
Working hard and playing harder
No matter what
Others should not really get to have a say
When you are not hurting anyone
To hell with them anyway
In this life people will come and go
Some are lessons learnt
While some stay all through the way
With all the highs and the lows
That gets thrown your way
This life is too short
Somethings are meant to be tossed
Out of your life any way
Like the saying goes
When one door closes
Other opens and paves the way
Accept what you cannot control
Make happiness your goal
Life is too short a journey
Why live it with regrets anyway
So go out and live life and seize the day

Baby who has seen tomorrow
So do borrow
A page of happiness from life
And fill it with all the colors of the rainbow
Baby why be so sad
When this world can be yours
Accept what you cannot control
And make happiness your goal
This life is after all too short a journey
So go live it with no regrets honey
If there is one lesson we should all takeaway
It spares no one
And comes everyone's way
A little bit of high
A little bit of low
Sometimes we have no choice
But to go with the flow
This life is after all too short a journey
So go live it with no regrets honey

Life is Meant to Be Lived with Regrets

When life feels like a dead end go out and touch someone
When life feels meaningless learn to let go and smile again
When life feels hopeless choose to be happy and live again
When everything around you feels like one big mess
Realize life will always be a little bit of love and little bit of regrets

Life is meant to be lived with regrets
It's ultimately about paying your due respects
Live life large like there's no tomorrow
Do not make choices which leads to sorrow
Few mistakes we all make are simply lessons learnt
Few we don't maybe opportunities lost and bridges burnt
If you do not take a chance on life you will never find out
Sometimes love is something you chase after instead of sitting it out
In this life things don't always come easy
Grab happiness from life even if it gets busy
In this world there are no guarantees in life
Take time to smell the roses and feel alive
Live life like it is meant to be conquered
Chase after your dreams and fulfil it and make it yours forever
Life will always come with ups and downs
Few highs and lows that will always come your way and meant to surmount
In this life sorrow is something nobody can escape
No matter where you hide or which path you take
People will give you rope to hang yourself
Learn to kick them hard and kick them back and respect yourself
Always face your fears head on no matter what and at life's every bend
Never ever surrender even if it is till the very end
What good is this life if you haven't lived it with regrets
It just means you have lived life and paid it it's due respect
When life feels like a dead end go out and touch someone
When life feels meaningless learn to let go and smile again
When life feels hopeless choose to be happy and live again
When everything around you feels like one big mess
Realize life will always be a little bit of love and little bit of regrets

Baby this Life is A Journey of Five Miles

Baby this life is a journey of five miles
Let's take these five steps together
While the sun smiles
Baby it's not like my life revolves around you
But facts and figures scream that I love you
Baby let's soar the skies together
Just give me a sign
Let's take it further
Baby this world is a strange chase
About you and I leaving a heavenly trace
Baby this life is nothing but destiny
So go ahead and set me free
Baby I am down on my knees
This to you is my silent plea
Baby please don't break my heart
You are my sunshine
My sweetheart
Baby when I put my arms around you
And tell you how much I love you
Don't think of it as a prison
Just surrender to this sweet sensation
And give my life a heavenly reason
Baby this world is a heavenly place
It's about you and me in this earthly space
Baby my heart belongs to you
So give me a clue
Let me take you higher
Trust me I am no liar
Where the lines between dreams and reality blur
It is you I have always been after
I just want to completely lose myself into you
Baby when I feel you around me
It chases away my blues
When I am with you no one in this world exists
It's just you and I with no twists
You and I are here forever
My love for you is the heavenly answer
Baby ever since you have come into my life
You have turned it topsy turvy and into a jive

I don't want to turn around and do an about face
After all there is no trace
Should we take it slow or fast
Forward or just simply backward at last
Or just feel free like a blue bird in the sky so vast
Baby let's soar above the white clouds
It's not like every day we are in our twenties
And we are all lost in the crowd
Baby what good are people around you
When they don't understand you
Baby believe me when I say this
Life with you is a sweet bliss
Baby when you are feeling lost when I am not around
Just connect the dots
And you will be on solid ground
Baby this world sometimes feels like it is in reverse gear
Just retrace your steps and do not fear
Baby when this world feels strange
And people feel stranger
Just think of me and you will remember
When it feels like this world is going
Upside down and to and fro
Think of me and take it slow
All your paths will lead to my heart
It was meant to set you free from the very start
Baby I am no rocket scientist
Is this dream just ashes, dust or reality
Baby this life is a journey of five miles
Let's take these five steps together
While the sun smiles
Baby it's not like my life revolves around you
But facts and figures scream that I love you
Baby let's soar the skies together
Just give me a sign
Let's take it further
Baby this world is a strange chase
About you and I leaving a heavenly trace

And Baby What's Love Anyway

Sometimes in this world of many
You meet someone
Who feels like your destiny
It feels like love from the very start
And down the road only to find out
It was not meant to last
And you ask yourself
And what's love anyway
When it does not last forever anyway
Like it was supposed to last
No matter how hard you try to make it stay
So why waste time over my broken heart
When love does not really last
And why call it love anyway
When love's not meant to last forever anyway

I am no Einstein
Laws of physics is not my dance
But it does not take a genius
To figure this one out
About love and romance
Love is not just once in a lifetime
And your only chance
Your only romance
To find love of your life
And happiness that comes by your side
As the only one sealed and dealed
And sent our way
It is not just about one
And only one love
And one and only one chance
But in this life
To give your heart another chance
To feel romance
And to feel it in different ways
In several different ways
Of beautiful people who will come into your life
In this life's journey
That we call life

At different points in different ways
In several different ways
And again a brand new chance at romance
And to define love once again
As a new happiness you feel in your life
In a sweet new beautiful way

I am no Einstein
And laws of physics is not my dance
And it does not take a genius
To figure this one out
About love and romance
To my broken heart
Which still sobs over love lost
Over love that has gone astray
To my aching heart
Which refuses to heal
From a wound that feels too deep
This is what I have to say
Why be this broken anyway
To my broken heart
Which still sobs over love lost
Over a love that has gone estray
To my aching heart
Which refuses to heal
From a wound that feels too deep
This is what I have to say
Why be this broken anyway
Once again I find myself
Consoling my broken heart
Which refuses to listen to reason
And feels so broken
That hurt won't go away
To pick up the pieces
And move on
It's not that life does not give you
A second chance
And a new romance
To feel whole new love
In a whole new way
And not just only one opportunity at love
That was sent sealed and dealt our way

So why be this broken anyway
In this life you do not get
Only one chance at romance
Is not what life and destiny
Has planned
For us anyway
In this world of many
We are destined to meet few and not just one
Who were created just for us
To start life as brand new
To meet someone new
As someone new to meet along the way
And not just one single chance at romance
Sent sealed and dealt our way

Poems of Love

It's Like Sands through the Hourglass

Like written in the stars it was before we came
Like words etched in stone that will never ever fade
It's like sands through the hourglass and this lonely summer skies
Things you cannot go back to and yet you cannot move on in life
No matter how hard you try
And this loneliness that stays with me as time passes me by
Like a lost lonely soul on this deserted lonely night
Like two lonely footprints in the sand that got washed away with tide
Like the love you lost and all those lonely nights you cried
Like coming home to a lonely house that feels like the cruel world outside
Knowing things are no longer the same trying hard to hide the pain inside
Once filled with hopes and dreams of love together you shared with pride
Seasons come and seasons go without a trace and pain you cannot hide
You don't notice a thing and your soul that feels lost and bared at this divide
Once again like a lost lonely soul on this deserted lonely night
Like two lonely footprints in the sand that just got washed away with tide
Like written in the stars it was before we came
Like words etched in stone that will never ever fade
It's like sands through the hourglass and this lonely summer skies
Things you cannot go back to and yet you cannot move on in life
No matter how hard you try
And this loneliness that stays with me as time passes me by

Seven Nights You and I

You and I
One night stand
Seven days Seven weeks
Seven oceans Seven seas
Seven into the night so serene
To smile together to die together
Every walk of life together
World may change always forever
Yet seasons all along meant not to be weathered
And in the end it did not matter
Honeymoon that never happened
Yet life that did
Apologies that never came
Forgive I couldn't and the inevitable
That was a long time coming
Life's high life low
It was for the two us to know
Some things not meant to be ignored
Still would have failed probably for sure
No matter which way we did go
Probably written in the stars and skies
Even before it was you and I
Complete opposites no way alike
Was meant to fail from the very first night
Thirteen years just one big lie
You and I
One night stand
Seven days Seven weeks
Seven oceans Seven seas
Seven into the night so serene

I Could Not Come and You Could Not Let Go - 1

I could not come
And you couldn't let go
Time passed us by
And sometimes life still feels like it is in a limbo
And we could not bring ourselves
To bridge this gap and our life that it still echoes
It still separates the two of us
And you are still no show
And no matter how hard I try
Sometimes I still wonder
Why is it that life turns out this way
Where it felt like
We were always meant to go our separate ways
I still remember the first time we met
I looked at your face
And I was swept away
And I knew that I wanted
Just to spend the rest of my life with you
With you by my side
That was my love's depth
And two weeks later
This promise that we kept
And tied the knot so sacred
And took the vows to spend forever
The rest of our lives together
We were so happy together
This life we had built for ourselves
Where just you and I existed
And nothing else mattered
And as time flew by
And before we knew it was five years
And together we wept
And together we cried
And here we are today
Nothing but complete strangers
In this strange town by the bay
That we once called our love getaway
Where once we could not
Think of life without each other
Even for a single day
Now here we are
Now nothing but strangers
Gone our separate ways

I Could Not Come and You Could Not Let Go - 2

I could not come
And you couldn't let go
Time passed us by
And sometimes life still feels like it is in a limbo
And we could not bring ourselves
To bridge this gap and our life that it still echoes
This bond that we once shared with each other
Never thought that
Anything could break what we had together
The way you cared and the way you were always there
Someone I could trust
Someone I could lean on
But destiny it seems had different plans all together
Never thought that one day
This storm will come into our lives
And we will get swept away
And end up going our separate ways
Always thought that our love was strong
That it would withstand the test of time
And would always survive (and hold strong)
And right the wrong
Yet here we are
With what once used to be our love
So young and so alive
Nothing left now but shattered dreams now
And heart that still often wonders
These years that have passed by
I still sometimes think of you
No matter how hard I try
This feeling that refuses to go away
Thinking about how it would have been
Between me and you
As seasons come and seasons go
And memories of you that still creeps up silently
Without my being aware of it
In this world and in this life
Where people and destiny
Are so entwined together
Yet some memories still so painful

That they simply refuse to fade or die
This feeling of loneliness that it brings with it
Of years together lost
Of love lost
Then you find yourself asking this question why?
When it was not meant to work out
And you knew this from the very start
Then why did you and I meet in the first place
And this feeling which even today
Simply refuses to fade or go away

If Only You Had Stayed

When I am all alone
I often find myself thinking of you
I close my eyes
And feel your lips on my lips
And a smile crosses my face
When I am all alone
I often find myself thinking of you
When ever I am at this familiar place
And I wonder how it would have been
If that night you had stayed
Whenever I am all alone
I often find myself thinking of you
And how it would have been
If that night you had stayed
That summer that we spent together
Where we couldn't keep our hands off of each other
Spending every moment together
Having the time of our lives
Before we went our separate ways
I often wonder how would it have been
If you had stayed
When I am all alone
I often find myself thinking of you
I close my eyes
And feel your lips on my lips
And a smile crosses my face
And I wonder how it would have been
If you had stayed
Whenever I am all alone
I often find myself thinking of you
And how it would have been
If that night you had stayed
Would you and I have still been completely into each other
Oblivious to the world where no one else mattered
Meaning everything to each other
Like two people who belonged together
Would you and I still have been best friends
That I would have loved sharing my life with
That I still loved coming home to every single day

Would you have been always my confidante
That I liked sharing my deepest secrets with
When l was having a rough day
Would you have been my soulmate like you used to
Would we have been there for each other
A shoulder to lean on
When this world was being a cold harsh place
Would you and I would have stayed in love
Just like that summer
Where we could not keep our hands off of each other
Hanging on to each others every word
Madly in love forever
No matter what life sent our way
If that night you had stayed
When I am all alone
I often find myself thinking of you
I close my eyes
And feel your lips on my lips
And a smile crosses my face
When I am all alone
I often find myself thinking of you
And how it would have been
If you had stayed

In this World of Millions

The breeze is gentle
The air smells nice
You and I lying on the grass
Your song softly singing in my head
And it reminded me of the first time
You kissed me
And I belonged to you
And you were mine
The skies were blue
The clouds so white
Trees all around
And nowhere to hide
The birds chirping
The flowers were blooming
The sun still comes out
But you are not there
And it once again reminds me of you
And I don't know why
There's people all around
Yet there's loneliness in the air
Something that seems to be missing from my life
What it is I do not know for sure
Even after all these years
Sometimes I think of you
And wonder how it would have been
If we had stayed together
Would my eyes still look for you
In every crowded room like it used to
Even after all this time

The branches of the trees
Spread out in front of me
In all of their majestic beauty
With beautiful green leaves of springtime
With their cool soothing shade
Out every single day without fail
Reminding me of your shoulders
I could always lean on when it got colder
That was always there for me

To escape from the harsh glare
Of the world outside
They say
In this world of millions
People come into your life in millions
Some to stay and some as passers by
And they say true love only comes once in a lifetime
Like a beautiful ray of sunshine
Of hope and happiness to grab from life
That only true and true love can define
And once again
Even after all these years
Sometimes I think of you
And wonder how it would have been
If we had stayed together
Would my eyes still look for you
In every crowded room like it used to
Even after all this time

Why is Life this Way

On a rainy day like this I find myself looking out of the window
The skies once again filled with black clouds
And the rain pouring down
And once again I find myself thinking
Without my wanting to my mind taking a walk down the memory lane
Always so painful that I don't know whether I should stay
Then you walk through my mind
And I cannot help but wonder how it would have been
If life had played out differently
Would I still want you in my life
And would I want you to hold on to me tight
Would we still have meant something to each other
I still remember the first time we met
I still remember every single thing you said
And once again I wonder
Why do things sometimes end up like this
There is chill in the air outside
How it used to be when we first met
When it used to be just you and I and no one else
And the world outside would cease to exist
And once again I wonder how it would have been
If you and I had not gone our separate way
In this world
Why is it sometimes
Love is about pain
Life about regrets
Family about hurt
Relationships about baggage
Strangers about kindness
And loneliness in the world
As I try to walk away I realize
Why does life sometimes turn out this way
In this world
Where your blood ties
Sometimes remind you it takes all kind
And strangers remind you
Kindness you sometimes find
In strange places
As I try to move on

Memories I try to leave behind
Hurt that life sent my way
Baggage I try to lose
So that the pain goes away
So that I no longer cry
Then once I realize
This world is sometimes
Just about people and their expectations
And things they have to say
That reminds you
Who we all are in this world and in our lives
Once again trying to move on
Once again trying to add some meaning to my life
Desperately trying to leave the hurt
Trying hard to make it work
In a world where life has a mind of its own
No matter how hard you try it still gets you
And let's you know
This world is one cruel place
This life that can be an unthinkable hurt
As you try to leave it all behind
As you try to move on in life
I once again wonder
Why is it sometimes
Love is about pain
Life about regrets
Family about hurt
Relationships about baggage
Strangers about kindness
And loneliness in the world

Baby the Beautiful Thing about Love

When I think about love
I am often reminded about this cruel irony about life
It makes you wonder
What's love anyway?
Love is an unnecessary hassle in life
Love is nothing but a compromise
Even in pain you have to smile
In love you have to fold
And pretend everything's all right
Who ever goes down the path of love
Never comes out of it in one piece or alive
Love gives you nothing but misery
Love gives you nothing but pain
In love you lose every time
Baby you are better off without love in life
Baby why would you want unhappiness
When you are better off keeping your distance then I find myself answering
my own question
And the most beautiful thing about love every time
What is life without love?
Without love life is meaningless
Without love life is merely about existing
Without love life is merely about breathing on earth
Person who has not found love is a very lonely man
Person who has not found love has a very empty life
Without love you are a lost soul
Baby no matter what they say
Everyone wants love in life
Baby no matter how much they run away
Everyone still secretly chases after love
Baby no matter how much you run scared
Love is something every heart needs
Baby no matter what you may say
Love is something we always crave
Because it is the life's most natural order
About happiness and what it should desire
Baby no matter how much you run away from it
Love is one thing every person will always want
Baby no matter how much you deny it

Love is what everyone secretly chases after
Baby the most beautiful thing
About love and about life
Love is the most beautiful fall
You can take in life
Your heart you may lose
Maybe even your mind
Yet everything inside of you
Screams you have won in life
Baby you may lose in love
But it is your heart you lose
And love that you do find
And the most beautiful win of your life
Love makes life beautiful
Love makes life feel like a celebration
Love decks your life with everything precious
Love brings all colors beautiful into your life
Love in its every form is what happiness feels like
Love makes this world a heavenly place
Every face of love makes this world beautiful
Love is the most beautiful feeling
Love is the most beautiful high
Love makes you feel good to be alive
Baby the way it makes you feel inside
Baby the way you feel to hold tight
Baby this life just feels like one beautiful high
And to realize
Love is the most beautiful fall to take in life
And that you can scream from top of the world
You have won in life
And once again everything inside of you
Telling you
You wanna scream
You have won in life
Baby the most beautiful thing
About love and about life
Love is the most beautiful high
And the most beautiful fall
You can take in life
Baby I don't understand why is it that you say no to love
It is the most beautiful high of life

Roses and Kisses Every Morning

Pancakes and roses every morning
To remind you of my love
Kisses and hugs till the sun comes down
To tell you
You I cannot get enough of
Our motto of no matter what
And at every cost
Always love and no war
And not going to bed mad
Or sleeping in separate beds
No matter what
Always waking up in each others arms
And hitting the snooze button
For extra five minutes on the alarm
Holding each other tight
And glad we kissed and made up
Simple things like the foods you cook
And laundry I fold as our daily chore
Hitting the shower together
Hoping to steal few extra moments of life with each other
And every other excuse we can find
To show our love
Our weekend getaways to the coast
To Downtown San Francisco
And world's every happiness for us to feel and know
To grab it no matter how future unfolds
As we kiss holding hands toes on ground
Oblivious to everything else around
Lovebirds who have found love and not want to be found
So in love and spellbound
As the passing cars honk by the only sound
It feels like you and I in someway grew up together
The way you came into my life like a breath of fresh air
And the way life got played out and we weathered
The way you taught me the meaning of love and all its colors
And how it feels to belong like two lovers
Every beautiful things you do and say
That reminds me how meaningful my life you make

Even in a room full of crowded people again today
You are the prettiest woman that takes my breath away
I fall more and more in love with you every day
The way you feel when I hold you tight
And the it always feels right
Tells me no matter what I can always call you mine

Baby There is Nothing I Won't Do to Be with You

Baby I wish you knew how much I love you
Baby I wish you knew how much I care for you
Baby I wish you knew How crazy I am about you
Baby I wish you knew I would move heaven and earth
Just to be with you
Baby there is nothing I won't do
Just to be with you
Baby I fell in love with you the day I laid my eyes on you
Baby there is nothing I won't do for you
Baby believe me when I tell you this
I love you deeply with my heart and soul
Baby believe me when I tell you this
I love you deeply with my every breath I take in this world
Baby I will climb the highest mountain
Baby I will dive the deepest ocean
Baby I will change the tides of the river
Just to be with you
Baby I will change the path of the wind
Baby I will weather the toughest storm
Baby I will make the sun rise in the west
Baby I will never let the moon hide in the clouds
Baby I will bring clouds down to earth
Baby I will fill the skies with shooting stars
Baby I will surf the highest waves
Just to be with you
Baby I will change the tide of time
Baby I will walk a thousand miles
Baby I will fly the seven seas and the Andes
Baby I will turn this world upside down
Baby I will walk on fire just to be with you
Just to be with you
Baby I will stop the seasons from changing
Baby I will stop the rain from falling
Baby I will stop the sun from setting
Just to be with you
Baby I will fill the landscape with beautiful fall colors all year round
Baby I will fill the landscape with first winter snow so pure and white
Baby I will bring the world to a standstill
Just to be with you

Baby I will stop the earth from rotating
Baby I will reinvent the wheel
Just to be with you
Baby I will change the way planets are aligned in the cosmos
Baby I will change the way stars are lined up in the universe
Baby I will turn this world into one beautiful music
Just to be with you
Baby I will fill your path with rose petals
Baby I will fill your world with new beginnings every morning
Baby I will fill the skies with white doves
Just to be with you
Baby I will move heaven and earth
Just to be with you
Baby I wish you knew how deeply
I love you
Baby I wish you knew how much I care for you
Baby I wish you knew How crazy I am about you
Baby I wish you knew I would move heaven and earth
Just to be with you
Baby there is nothing I won't do Just to be with you
Baby there is nothing I won't do Just to be with you
Baby you live in my heart and you're my soul
Baby you are every breath I take and my world
Baby believe me when I tell you this
I have always loved you
Baby I wish you knew I would move heaven and earth
Just to be with you

The World through Your Eyes

When this life feels like one complicated maze and a never ending chase
I am so glad you came into my life
Because you make my world a beautiful place
When this life feels like one complicated maze and a never ending chase
I am so glad you came into my life
Because you give my life new meaning every single day
To give my life the meaning of love
That has been known to every lover on this earth
Since the beginning of days
That only Romeo and Juliet's romance and love can say
Whenever I see the world through your eyes
Everything in my world falls in place
Whenever I see the world through your eyes
This world feels like a heavenly place
Whenever I see the world through your eyes
Dots connect and this universe makes sense once again
Whenever I see the world through your eyes
I am no longer all alone in this strange world and I have a someone to lean on again
Whenever I see the world through your eyes
I know I have someone in this world to call all mine again
Whenever I see the world through your eyes
Happiness feels within reach and I say a silent prayer again today
Whenever I see the world through your eyes
This emptiness I feel like something has been missing from my life for a very
very long time goes away
Whenever I see the world through your eyes
I realize that sometimes strangers are meant for each other
And no matter where life took us
Life was waiting for us to meet one day
Whenever I see the world through your eyes
I now know what love feels like
The way you and I were supposed to know it
In our hearts and in every single way
And then I close my eyes and take a deep sigh and visualize your face
And then I close my eyes and take a deep sigh and visualize your face
And realize that you make my world a perfect place
And then I close my eyes and take a deep sigh and visualize your face
And then I close my eyes and take a deep sigh and visualize your face
And realize that you make my world a perfect place

I am so glad you came into my life
You make my world a beautiful place
I am so glad you came into my life
You give my life new meaning every single day
To give my life the meaning of love
That has been known to every lover on this earth
Since the beginning of days
That only Romeo and Juliet's romance and love can say

Way I Feel about You

The way you smile at me
I know life sang a beautiful song to me when I was lost somewhere
The way your face lights up whenever you see me
Tells me how much you care
The way you always believe in me when I need you
When this world feels like a forsaken prayer
Every little things you do for me
Tells me what I have in you is rare
Our love that always stays strong
Even when life feels like a despair
When I am having the worst day of my life
You remind me I have you and the love we share
The way it feels when I see your sweet face and hold you
Like I have my best friend and my soul I can bare
With you in my life everything seems to fall in place
And this world feels like a beautiful affair
A sign from above you and I are meant to be together
Always forever and not just a passing fare
Even when everything feels lost and I am losing my religion
I love you for the way you are always there
And no matter what
You will always be there
And the way I feel about you
And our love that holds so true
No matter how much we fight it's still always you
And when it feels like nothing about this world holds true
The way I can always come home to you
As someone who understands me the way you do
And I just want to hold you
And kiss you
Until the morning sun rises in crimson hue
And never ever let go of you

If I Can Have You in My Life

When I don't see you
My life is just not the same
And I look for you
In every crowd and every face
When I see you
You give me a reason to smile
And this world feels like a beautiful place
With you by my side
When I think of you
It feels like you were created just for me
And nothing else matters
And when you are not there
My world shatters
Because you are not mine
You don't know this
But ever since the first time I saw you
I have been in love with you
You don't know this
Ever since the first time I saw you
I have wanted to make you mine
Like you and I belong together
And nothing else exists

If I can have you
I promise you I will not ask for
Anything else
If I can have you
I promise you I will love you
More than life itself
If I can have you
I promise you I will break off all ties
With the rest of the world
If I can have you
I promise you will be my only religion
In the whole wide world

If I can have you
I promise you I will
Never make you cry

If I can have you
I promise you no harm will come your way
Till the day I die
If I can have you
I promise you I will change
The blues in the sky
If I can have you
I promise you I will change the tides
Of the roaring ocean highs

If I can have you
I promise you I will
Change the course of the winds
Just to have you in my life
If I can have you
I promise you I will follow you anywhere
Come rain or shine
If I can have you
I promise you I will have
Bed of roses in your path wherever you go
If I can have you
I promise you that I will make
Heaven shower flowers on you
Like a blessing from above

If I can have you
I promise you I will make sure
The rainbow in the sky is upside down
As a beautiful smile always on your face
For me to see
If I can have you
I promise you I will always make sure
Your life is sun kissed
Like the sun smiles only for you and me
If I can have you
I promise you I will never abandon you
No matter what comes by
If I can have you
I promise you I will come chasing after you
No matter which part of the world you hide

If I can have you
I promise you I will have
The clouds for you to walk on
At your feet
If I can have you
I promise you
I will steal all the happiness in the world
And lay it at your feet
(And make it your life)
If I can have you
I promise you
Nobody can ever take you away from me
That is how deep my love runs for you
If I can have you
I promise you
Even God will not be able to
Break the bond between us
That is how deep my love runs for you
And always will
Till the day I die

If I can have you
I promise you
I will make sure no one ever hurts you
And not a single tear ever runs down your eyes
As long as I am alive
If I can have you
I promise you
No harm ever comes your way
I will protect you from the coldest winter days
With you in my arms
Protecting you always

When I don't see you
My life is just not the same
And I look for you
In every crowd and every face
When I see you
You give me a reason to smile
And this world feels like a beautiful place
With you by my side
When I think of you

It feels like you were created just for me
And nothing else matters
And when you are not there
My world shatters
Because you are not mine
You don't know this
But ever since the first time I saw you
I have been in love with you
You don't know this
Ever since the first time I saw you
I have wanted to make you mine
Like you and I belong together
And nothing else exists

You Can Kiss Me Anytime - 1

You can kiss me anytime
Because you tug at my heart
You can kiss me anytime
Because you speak to my soul
You can kiss me anytime
The way it feels when you hold tight
You can kiss me anytime
Because you always do it right
When your lips touch my lips
You always make me smile
Kiss me in my sleep
Kiss me in my dreams
Kiss me all night long
Kiss me until the dawn
Kiss me when I am awake
Kiss me when I am in a daze
Kiss me when I am sleep walking
Kiss me to shut me up when I am talking
Kiss me when I am looking hot
Kiss me when I have just rolled out of bed
Kiss me when I am serious
Kiss me when I am teasing
Kiss me when I am hurting
Kiss me when I am flirting
Kiss me when it is about love
Kiss me even when it not about sex
Kiss me tip toeing on your toes
Kiss me holding hands very close
Kiss me to wake me up every morning
Kiss me just to say that you love me darling
You can kiss me anytime
Because you tug at my heart
You can kiss me anytime
Because you speak to my soul
You can kiss me anytime
The way it feels when you hold tight
You can kiss me anytime
Because you always do it right
When your lips touch my lips

You always make me smile
Kiss me for no reason
Kiss me in every changing season
Kiss me when it is stormy
Kiss me when it is calm
Kiss me in the pouring rain
Kiss me in the winter snowflakes
Kiss me when the sun shines
Kiss me when I am soaked
Kiss me when I am happy
Kiss me when I am sad
Kiss me when I am naughty
Kiss me when I am nice
Kiss me to make me stay
Kiss me so that I never walk away
Kiss me when I am in my woolen mittens
Kiss me in the moonlight until I am smitten
Kiss me barefoot at the beach
Kiss me with abandonment on top of the tallest building
Kiss me until I am breathless
Kiss me just to say you love me

Baby I Am Right Where You Left Me

Baby when you are feeling lost
And you want to get out of it at all cost
And this world feels like it's upside down
And you feel like you just want to drown
Just remember my kiss inside out
Let it rock you to and fro and about
And give this world a big shout
Baby when you are feeling lost
And you want to get out of it at all cost
Just retrace all your steps
And all your paths will lead to my doorstep
With me right where you left me
With open arms to set you free
Baby this life is nothing but destiny
Where you and I were meant to be
Baby this world is a maze
Where sometimes everything feels like a haze
Go fly I am setting you free
If you really love me
You will come back to me
As you soar the skies so high
You will remember the way
I used to kiss you inside out
And it made you cry
I still remember the way we would make love
It was like a blessing from above
I still remember the first time we met
You were in your twenties
In a little black dress
I was completely swept
I remember the first time
Our lips touched
I could feel the blood rushing
Into my head like a gush
My world turned completely upside down
And my life turned into a smile
From a frown
Baby this love is a strange thing
Joy and sadness it does bring

How can something that gives us so much happiness
Can also be a pain offspring
Baby it is a prison we just cannot escape
Hard as we may try
It still takes its own shape
Baby do not feel dejected
We have all been rejected
Who hasn't seen sadness in life
No matter how hard we strife
It is like afterlife
Baby when you are feeling confused and lost
Just think of me when all your avenues exhaust
We are star crossed lovers for sure
We belong to each other in richness and poor
In this world strangers sometimes feel like our own
And facts and figures does get blown
Baby I am not a rich man or a genius
I am just firmly grounded
And my love for you is aces
Baby please do accept
My love for you has that depth
Baby when you are feeling lost
And you want to get out of it at all cost
And this world feels like it's upside down
And you feel like you just want to drown
Just remember my kiss inside out
Let it rock you to and fro and about
And give this world a big shout
Baby when you are feeling lost
And you want to get out of it at all cost
Just retrace all your steps
And all your paths will lead to my doorstep
With me right where you left me
With open arms to set you free
Baby this life is nothing but destiny
Where you and I were meant to be

On this Strange Lonely Night

We went our separate ways
Now we are miles apart
We both did everything we could
To forget each other
Yet even after all these years
On this strange lonely night
I find myself thinking about you
And wonder why is it sometimes
That two people come into each other's life
When it is not meant to last
It is true that you are not with me
It is true that I am not with you
Even miles apart from each other
I once again find myself thinking about you
On this strange lonely night
Once again thought of you crossed my mind
How even in the darkness of our lives
You were the one I used to reach out to
And I was the one you could always lean on
This pact we had with each other
Even with the miles between us
Today in the loneliness of the night
I thought I heard you thinking about me
I thought I heard you call my name
There was a time when we had this unspoken connection
And strangely felt this ache
And once again I thought to myself
Do we still have this unbreakable connection
That we once had each other
Which no distance between us could erase
No matter which force of the universe tried
The sun still comes up
The moon still shines
The birds still chirp
And you are no longer mine
Everything is still the same
And everything is on time
Yet sometimes it still feels
Something is missing from my life

I no longer know who is to blame
Maybe we could have had it all
Maybe we could have stayed
Instead of assuming love had died
Maybe you should not have run away
Maybe I should have heard your cries
Maybe we should both have cared
And not run scared
And allow life happen the way it did happen
To both of us
If only life had not happened
And we had cared
Somethings in life maybe are meant to be
In my heart it was always you and I
If only life had not happened
Maybe we should not have despaired
And maybe you should not have run scared
There is nothing together
We could not have overcome
If only you had cared
Maybe you should have given us a chance
After all life is not about running scared
This is not a complaint
This is not a dare
Either to you or to life
Mind still goes there
And wonders why is it sometimes
Things are not meant to be
No matter how much you do care
When together there is nothing we could not have weathered or conquered
Maybe we should have been patient
Maybe we would have found out
Whether love would have seen us through
And how much we may have cared
I know that we have gone our separate ways
And things are beyond repair
But I still cannot help thinking about us
About the life that we once shared
And maybe we should have stayed together
And maybe we would have found out
If love would have seen us through
And how much we may have cared

Poems of Faith

Love and How it Still Works
(On Live and Life)

It does not matter how you do meet each other in this world
called life or why

When it feels like a beautiful song of life why ask why

The simple truth of math and science is how it still works in
life and will always apply

Whether it is as an irresistible attraction or an instant high or
just love at first sight

Or strange idyllic summer afternoon of just strangers passing by
and an intense liking you just cannot deny

Love and life still ends up being about two strangers who were
destined to meet each other in this loneliness of night called life

Love will still be about grabbing a moment from life and
making happiness their most beautiful high of life

This world is a strange place where every blueprint tells you
love is one of the happiness of life

Life still goes on and even when you don't miss it you still
know something is missing in life

Life does not come to a standstill and yet it feels like maybe
love is something beautiful to have in life

Without love the days are short and the nights are long life
feels empty and this city a ghost town where happiness died

Yet no matter who you are or what you are it is one thing most
difficult to find

Life which has a mind of its own that keeps you busy and occupied
and many reasons you have given it as your beautiful highs

Love no matter how hard you chase after it it still feels like
one quintessential lie

No matter how hard you run away from it when you are
hurting you still cannot hide

No matter how much you have told yourself your happiness
through another person will never ever get defined

You even tell yourself not even in a million years will you
bother with love no matter how lonely you feel tonight

And then you see two people in love and your mind takes you
back to that place and makes you smile

It's such an incredibly beautiful feeling to feel and to have in
life you once again realize

Love you are a mystery and when I find you I hope you are the
most beautiful feeling of my life

Trying to Make Sense of it All

Two lonely souls in this world
You can tell from their face
Had the worst news of their life
It was this feeling
That everything was lost
Don't know a thing about each other
Yet need a shoulder to cry
At the worst place of their life
Trying to make sense of it all
Life once again has come to a full circle
Once again it had something to say
Just when I thought I had it all
Someone to hold on to tight
It was all lost in one single night
Like the storm of my life
That came into my life without warning
All lost in one night
Life once again reminding me
What I had once thought was love
To last forever
That life had sung to me
Turned out to be all in my head
Left all alone with my broken heart
Once again all alone in this world
To heal trying to make sense of it all
Tears that won't stop
This treachery that I feel
Tears that just won't stop
As it rolls down my eyes
Feeling sorry for myself
Even there cannot escape or hide
No matter how many tears I shed
Desperately trying to wipe them away
Still cannot console my broken heart
Which weeps once again
At this betrayal I feel inside
That life has left me with
Left at this crossroad once again
Completely confused and lost

Once again trying to make sense of it all
To make the hurt go away
Trying to pick up the pieces
Still cannot stop this feeling
I feel inside like all is lost
And I weep for myself again today
Once again what life had to say
Things I cannot look back at
Things I cannot change
What's left now is just ashes
Of what used to be my life
Cannot make the pain go away
Yet I know life stops for nobody
Despite this catastrophe
And to simply know
Where life has once again brought me
And this treachery that I feel
That we sometimes call life
And this hurt that just won't go away
This sense of disbelief
This disquiet I feel within
As my heart weeps
Like a cry from my soul
Which is still searching
Like a cry from my soul
Crying out for help
At what was lost
And my heart which refuses to heal
As I once again
Try to wipe away the tears
As it silently rolls down my face

The Rarest of Rare Religion

Nothing in this world could faze him, not even scared of God
as what he took on in this world

Always faced life with boldness and conquered with heart like a
force that could not be stopped

Yet whenever he was in his presence he could not help but
wonder what did it ultimately mean after all

And in the silence of his brain and quietness of his life he could
not bear to see his own reflection and what it said

And this head that would not bow to any force in this
universe would bow humbly to his might as religion that he
was in this universe

These eyes that were never filled with shame about the religion
we were in the house of God yet pangs of conscience and face
of regret to him he humbly was

The rarest of rare religion that you then get to see as he realizes
what's right and what's wrong

The flagship you would have fired yet what you admired and
this universe that sometimes can be one big noise

Where it is sometimes difficult to separate facts and our
ignorance of the unknown and our innocence about the known
entwine and the way the truth gets lost

Our belief system that makes us who and what we happen to
be in this universe and yet things we have always known for
sure even with the obvious staring us in the face

About the Walks We Walk

The temptation that's thrown our way
The thoughts that crosses our mind
Mind that wanders
Brain that ponders
Intentions that waiver
Reasons that blur
It's still about the walks we walk
Defining who we are
As things that we choose
As things we do
As intelligence and religion we are
As religion that holds true

Tears we have cried about life that happened
Hurt that still stays despite since then what happened
Crosses we bear
Regrets we share
Souls we bare
People that care
It's still about the walks we walk
Defining who we are
As things that we choose
As things we do
As intelligence and religion we are
As religion that holds true

Sounds Like What He Has to Say

When it feels like he says it with our gene pool called our DNA
As a gift from him even before we were even born as
decisions already made

When it feels like he says it as life as one big chess game
As things he sends our way as lessons in life that was sent our way

When it feels like he says it as life's highs and lows when this
world feels like a cruel harsh place
As things we do in life and the curve balls we do avoid and the
paths that we do take

When it feels like he says it as things I choose to do in life as
who we are with all our passions in life every new day
As things we do in life defining as as who we are in this
universe and happiness it makes

When it feels like when he says it as the way I believe in him
and religion I do not forsake
As in God we choose to believe in even when we are at the
hardest place

When it Comes to Life

This life that is sometimes a story of pain and sorrow
This life that is sometimes a story of love and sweetness and tomorrow
One thing though will always stay
You neither can quit nor run away

When it comes to life
And our gloomiest day
And our darkest hour
Our mind works in strangest ways
And the deepest cut
Like an unbearable pain
That God sent our way
Of wounds it does create

What once felt like life as usual
Filled with love and laughter
That nobody could take away
Turned out to be one big lie
Of my blissfully ignorant life
Waiting for the right moment
Just to be played
Your whole world turned upside down
Everywhere you turn
The hatred you feel inside
Or just for the person whose religion
Just got played

This life that is sometimes a story of pain and sorrow
This life that is sometimes a story of new beginnings and tomorrow
One thing though will always stay
You neither can quit nor run away

Life and its Ups and Downs and the Rocky Road that Comes Along

When life just feels perfect and about new hope and filled with
new promises and nothing that can possibly go wrong
When you just want to celebrate life and something it has to
say tonight and something to hold on to all life long
Then it feels like you are all alone in this world and not a
shoulder to cry on or a single soul to lean on
When life feels hopeful and full of new beginnings and you just
want to stay up all night long to see the sunrise at dawn
It is cold outside and you need something to warm you up from
the chill in the air you feel in your bones until it's gone
You can't get your mind off of things as life keeps taking you
there about things you lost along the way and memories that
still linger on all hurt and torn
Soul food day for my bruised soul as life is being mean and
exhaustion that you feel and mind that still needs to stay strong
You are with your best friend and you have something to be
thankful for like life has finally sung an incredibly beautiful song
When it feels like one of those days where murphy's law is in
full force taking its swing and all lines are drawn
When life feels like a beautiful love story with a beautiful ending
and that you were born to win since the day you were born

In the Darkness of the Night

Higher in money
Higher in religion
Yet this religious shits of my life
Had such a beautiful story to tell
In the darkness of the night
You once again realize
What is life after all
When everyone in life
Turns out to be beauty
With an innate sense of ride
Their colored skin pride
Their injured voice
In the darkness of the night
You feel raped of your rights
You try to ignore it all
It still won't go away
You try to turn away
Yet it still stays
Once again it repeats itself
Like a story it has to tell
You try to look at the picture
Like a picture for hell
Yet it feels framed and sized
Something that feels familiar
Like some story of my life
Which won't go away
No matter how hard I try
It will say what it has to say
Until it has written itself
Once again today

Straight from the Heart

Love was my playground I invited you to leading to the path to my heart

Yet you always chose to disbelieve and player you were from the very start

Love was my playground I invited you to leading to the path to my heart

Yet games was your playground and player you were from the very start

The excuses life gives you as things you cannot allow to slide

The reasons life gives you as a clause from your distant past

The rarest of rare religion of people's life that you are straight from the heart

Things that you already do know and the religion that you are that tears them apart

All the reasons you have anyway to be who you are in the darkest hour

About that cold day of life and things no matter how hard you try you cannot forget

About the human bankruptcy you happen to be and the way one mistrusts

Somethings that then does gets written on the pages of the subconscious

The wall that then builds in your mind about strings that now no one can touch

Reasons that you no longer can justify no matter what you may mean to me
now as I put the past to rest

The rarest of rare religion of people's life that you are that I never did except

Things that I do know now and the religion that you are in life when life is a tempest

Then I move on trying not to look back at who you were in my life since
the very first time we met

Love was my playground I invited you to leading to the path to my heart

Yet you always chose to disbelieve and player you were from the very start

Games were always your playground and a player you were straight from the heart

Our Life and Our Roots
(The Way People Lay Their Roots in Their Own Rights in this World)

Once again I am feeling restless and find myself in front of my
window looking outside and thinking to myself why is it that
life sometimes turns out the way it does

The sun is about to set and there is crimson and gray hues all
over the horizon far away in the distance where the sky meets
the land hidden between the trees as far as the eye can see

And I wonder in this life how much of it is really in our hands
and how much of it is fate where no matter how hard you try
there are certain things we just cannot change

My eyes then fall on the majestic tree in front of me and it has
all the beautiful shades of the setting sun reflecting off of it in
all its majestic colors of the skies and azure in the dusk light

The tree has almost been here forever now and lost in my
thoughts I get distracted once again and wonder when this
tree was planted and the way it always seems that silently has
a thousand stories to tell

It feels like just like me it has seen several gruesome seasons
and weathered several storms along the way and stands tall with
some stories it has to tell about life and what came our way
without warning in our lives

I sometimes wish it could actually talk because it always stands
so tall in its majestic beauty that pulls me towards it in its grace
that is always completely breathtaking

For sometime now it has become an important part of my life
and the hours I spend in front of it reflecting about life in front
of this window and about life's intricacies and mysteries that it
holds within it as a puzzle

Whenever I look at this tree I sometimes think I identify
with it as what we both have weathered in this life and in our

silence alone have something important to say about Life and the way life happens to so many of us

Or maybe our stories are even more similar than the first simple dissection of the of life than I am aware of or maybe it's just the way it stands tall reminding me of the way life sometimes plays out no matter what and you have no choice but to fight it out

It is like the roots of this tree which reminds you that what really determines in this life who and what you are and how tall you stand in this life are your very own roots and not just the roots you come from but actually the roots lay in life in life as intelligence and religion you are in life

And it makes you realize that in your life your youth and past are shaped by the seasons that come into your life which then shapes to a great extent the way we do do things in life

And the decisions we do make and the way we deal with life then ends up shaping us as who and what we are today despite life's cold cruelties that sometimes comes our way

And then I realized that at certain point in our life we all have to make this transition in life where it stops being about the roots we came from and becomes about the roots that we ourselves have laid as every single thoughts to every single decisions that we have made that defines as who and what we are in this world today

It then becomes about us as an individual that we are and these roots that we have laid with the religion we have chosen to practice in life that then becomes our very own identity in this life

It reflects the weathers we have stormed just like this majestic tree in front of me which has probably seen as many seasons as I have which now feels like my very own identity as to what we both have to say in life

It also makes you realize that few things in life that we have always taken for granted in life and if for some reason life does not turn out to be that way it is like this tree standing silently in front of me not saying a word yet says a thousands of stories to me about how life is and has this one very important thing it has to say to me

That in life sometimes a total stranger can come into your life and give your life that meaning which life sometimes takes away from you as few things you always thought you could count on in life

I realized that that then gives us that true meaning that we have all been looking for in life to stand tall just like this majestic tree in front of me as the seasons and weathers we have stormed that came into our lives and shaped us who and what we are today

What has now become a morning ritual to spend sometime looking outside this window and reflecting on life I once again realize that it is like feeding the soul and realizing that a long time ago it stopped being about anything other than the roots we lay and no longer about the roots we come from

And that when one door closes another door opens as something beautiful that life has to say with the roots we have created for ourselves with what we have made of ourselves in this life as who we are in this life

And then I am reminded how every morning the first thing I see is the first ray of the sun hitting the tree and catching the drops of water on the leaves

It is like a sign of new beginning and new hope that each new day brings with it as what life should mean to each and everyone of us and the way it is meant to be lived

I No Longer Feel Alone

This vast open promising skies
With its mesmerizing hold and ties
Pulls me towards itself
Like a magnet to a shell
I feel free I feel at home
I am no longer by myself
I no longer feel alone
I look at this magnificent view
It seems to be saying to me
That I love you
And all I want to do is behold its beauty
And say I love you too

The mountains so high and majestic
It fills me with awe and it's absolutely fantastic
Big, strong and mighty
And O so mysterious
It has a power over me that leaves me breathless
As I shout out to the mighty mountains
It echoes my voice back like a fountain
It seems to be saying to me
That I love you
And all I want to do is
Hug this imposing beauty
And say I love you too

The wind is blowing strong and gentle
The breeze is flowing soft like an angel
Making the trees swing to and fro
This ethereal feeling that I just don't want to let go
As the leaves fall against my cheeks
I feel humbled and O so meek
The gentle breeze blowing through the trees
It seems to be saying to me
That I love you
And all I want to do is
Dance with the breeze
And say I love you too

The birds of a feather
They have all flocked together

Singing in unison
Feels like a beautiful crimson
In the morning sun
It feels like music to my senses
And I no longer care about the consequences
It seems to be saying to me
That I love you
And all I want to do is
Is lose myself in this moment
And say I love you too

This beautiful heavenly sunshine
Falling on this open space and fierce race
Imposing trees and O so music to the ears
Singing birds and bees
They all set my heart free
As the sun shines down upon me
I feel blessed
My soul feels sun kissed
It simply makes me feel cozy and warm
I know I can weather any storm
As long as I stay strong
I spread my arms
And look at the skies above me
And it seems to be saying to me
That I love you
And all I want to do
Is kiss it back
And say I love you too

As I am lost in this beauty
Of the rivers and the mountains
It beckons me to itself in its wide bastion
And whispers in my ears
I want to be your friend so sincere
I won't share this secret with the flowers and the trees
Or for that matter with anybody
You and I belong together
Together we will be bold and conquer
I just want to climb the majestic mountains so high
I can feel the sheer love and pure joy
You are my happiness and my sunshine
Will you be my friend
If you don't mind

Ode to the Torrential Rain
(About Life and the Way it Happens to Several of Us Like it Has a Mind of its Own)

It has been pouring all day long like hell hath no fury with strong gust of winds refusing to die down

It feels like a tropical monsoon cyclone coming from the mountains of Pacific Northwest

Or maybe the Sierra Nevada desert depositing all the water on earth in one single day

The skies had been scattered with deafening thunderstorms and lightning all night long like an ominous message of things to come

There is a somber feeling in the air with glooming threatening clouds that is covering the horizon which refuses to abate or subside

I have this sinister feeling that it will probably bring with it a very cold front with it from the Savannah Climes

I could hear the winds howling and the gutters and the storm drains rattling and the trees that seem to about to give way with a terminal velocity that is rarely ever seen

The heavy rain feels like the tundra polar ice cap has melted on the great plains of subtropical ridge

And flooded the entire landscape for not a soul to venture out on a forsaken day like this

I can hear the rain pounding against the window and I look outside with apprehension

I look up at the skies above which still looks foreboding and think to myself that maybe the skies are finally clearing up a little and showing signs of letting up

And as I look up anxiously once again I can almost see the
sun shining through

All day long it has been without a hint of silver lining or
white anywhere in the skies

The rain still seems to be coming down hard and is relentless as
it pounds the ground and there is still no sign of it coming to a
standstill anytime soon

And then I find myself looking up once again to see if I can
trace its origin in the skies right where it all starts back to the
clouds where it is originating from

And as far as my eyes can see I am not able to see it that
high up no matter how hard I try

I then look a little further down into the distance and a
beautiful pattern begins to emerge

I could see one smooth flow of torrential rain and what we call
rainfall as it hits the ground and no matter how hard I try I
cannot take my eyes off of it as it continues to hit the ground

And I find myself completely fascinated as I watch it contact
the ground and form small rippling droplets of water

As I look a little closer they look like little small crystals strewn
in the path ahead of me like a blanket of endless crystals of
diamonds all around me

And once again they remind me of pure white prisms creating
all the colors of the rainbow right here on ground

Like someone decided to bring the rainbows from the skies
above down on earth

And I find myself completely mesmerized and as I look at this
breathtaking sight in front of me

I cannot help but admire it's beauty in its pure simplicity

Feels Good to Be Free

Not a care in the world
Not a dime in my name
But what the hell
Life has come to a full circle again
Is this what it feels like to be free
I never knew my heart all along held the key

I just want to flee
From this crazy city
And feel the wide open road ahead
Which tells me why be sad but be free
The clouds humbly touching the sea
The beautiful sight leaves a silent plea
On my lips which wants to welcome the rain
O what a beautiful feeling in my veins
Don't wake me up if I am dreamin
I just feel like throwing my head back and screamin
And tell the whole world it feels good to be free
This vast wide open skies, sea and me

As the wind blows through my hair
And the skies are crystal clear and fair
The warm sunshine on my face
And dew drops in my hair
Go ahead world
See if I care
As I feel the big blue sea
Which beckons me
To spread my arms wide
And feel the sunshine
As it shines down upon my face
I feel nature's kiss and grace

The soft sand underneath my feet
As the water gushes back into the sea
The waves hitting my face
Makes my heart race
The salty spray of water on my lips
Makes my heart flip

I just want to fly
Into this wide open sky
As I look at the big blue skies
I am just glad I am alive
And I am glad I did not take the dive

I feel my soul sing a song
Nothing can possibly go wrong
This warm and fuzzy feeling I feel all over
To be one with nature
And gentle breeze blowing all over
Lord please have mercy
Please don't stop
I just want to feel crazy
This I can say with certainty
This is how life is supposed to feel

As I longingly look at the skies
My soul just wants to soar and fly
At the beauty as far as my eyes can see
I am glad it is this heavenly place and me
Life you better not be mocking me
As I lustfully soak you up and feel the joy and glee
In this heavenly place
In this heavenly moment
Life certainly feels like a poetry

Not a care in the world
Not a dime in my name
But what the hell
Life has come to a full circle again
Is this what it feels like to be free
I never knew my heart all along held the key

Life's Journey

Another day
New beginning
Sun came up
Stars did shine
Clouds smiled too
Night so poignant
And you were not here
Life's journey
Another mile
A journey so long
Weathered song
Hurt inside
You try to hide
World full of people
Yet strangers they are all
Faces you see
In inhuman forms
You turn away
Memories linger on
Plenty you try to erase
It's like it's written
On your subconscious page
Hard as you may try
You cannot shake it away
You try to put it behind
Like a painful memory
It still stays
You try to move on
Yet like a baggage
It simply refuses to go away
Once again you wonder
What is it about life
No matter what you are
The way it will still play
What the other person
Does have to say
How deep is the cut
It's still up to us
This world is not an island
And this life you cannot escape

Resources

If you or someone you know is facing or living through homelessness, please reach out to one of the following organizations:

Feeding Tampa Bay – Trinity Café
https://feedingtampabay.org/ways-we-serve/trinity-cafe

Blanket Tampa Bay
https://www.blanketampabay.org/

The Homeless Voice
855-92-HELP-1

Do You Want to Make an Impact?

NOW Publishing will help you build your book and deliver your message in a powerful, impactful way.

Everyone has a story to tell and NOW Publishing is here to help them bring those stories to life. Whether you have already written a book and need a marketing partner to promote your story, or have an idea for a book that can change lives and inspire others, we are here to help you turn that into something memorable and marketable.

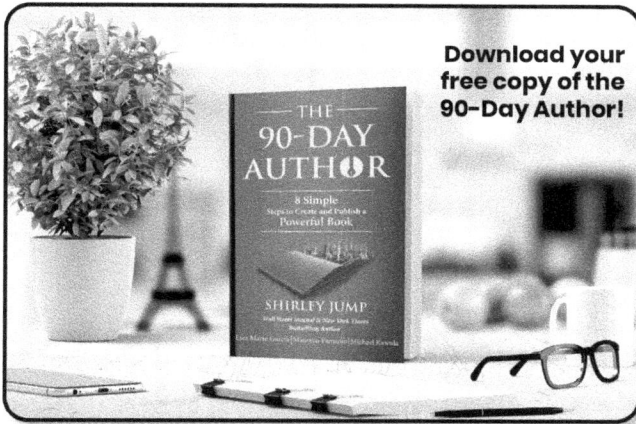

Download your free copy of the 90-Day Author!

THE
90-DAY
AUTHOR

8 Simple Steps to Create and Publish a Powerful Book

SHIRLEY JUMP

About the Author

Sabita Mishra was born in Munger, Bihar on May 26, 1967. Her childhood days were in Jamshedpur, Bihar, in the Northern part of India where her dad was an Engineer and a Chief Technology Officer working for a major iron and steel company called TATA Steel, and her mom was a homemaker. In 1989, she moved to the USA to a small town in Illinois called Urbana-Champaign where her husband was doing his PhD in finance at the University of Illinois. After a few years in Illinois as a homemaker, she decided to go back to school and completed her bachelor's degree in Chemical Engineering at the University of Illinois. She then worked for several high-tech companies on the West Coast. A few years ago, when facing homelessness, she took up writing and writing poems in her free time became her way of dealing with life. This is her first book and is a collection of poems and talks about life's highs and lows and how to find courage and hope at times like these, and come out of it stronger.

To read more poetry and connect with the author, visit: LifeDisarranged.com

www.ingramcontent.com/pod-product-compliance
Lightning Source LLC
Chambersburg PA
CBHW070817100426
42742CB00012B/2386